W9-BOB-355

DATE DUE

DEMCO 38-297

SLOVENIA

Ted Gottfried

BENCHMARK BOOKS

MARSHALL CAVENDISH
NEW YORK

PICTURE CREDITS
Cover photo: © Peter Turnley/CORBIS
AFP: 27, 29, 31, 33, 34, 41, 45, 107 • ANA Press Agency: 14, 51, 53, 56, 58, 59, 63, 66, 67, 70, 73, 74, 104, 105, 106 • Camera Press: 130 • Corbis Inc.: 18, 21, 23, 25, 28, 37, 40, 77, 108, 120 • Focus Team Italy: 6, 30, 35, 39, 42, 48, 68, 80, 81, 82, 99, 129 • HBL Network Photo Agency: 43, 88, 109 • Kodia Photo & Graphis: 69, 87, 89, 92, 93, 97, 119, 131, 71, 101 • Life File Photos: 4, 75, 84, 90, 94, 95, 98, 114, 115, 126 • Lonely Planet Images: 1, 9, 36, 38, 46, 49, 54, 55, 57, 60, 61, 62, 65, 72, 78, 83, 102, 110, 113, 116, 117, 125 • Panos Pictures: 52, 91, 123, 124 • Still Pictures: 10, 64, 86, 128 • Audrius Tomonis/www.banknotes.com: 85, 135 • Topfoto: 5, 19, 22

ACKNOWLEDGMENTS
Thanks to Gordon N. Bardos, Assistant Director, Harriman Institute, Columbia University, for his expert reading of this manuscript.

PRECEDING PAGE
An old church that stands on an island located in the middle of Lake Bled is a scenic spot to take in the beauty surrounding one of Slovenia's most popular lakes.

Marshall Cavendish Benchmark
99 White Plains Road
Tarrytown, NY 10591
Website: www.marshallcavendish.us

© Marshall Cavendish International (Asia) Private Limited 2005
® "Cultures of the World" is a registered trademark of Marshall Cavendish Corporation.

Series concept and design by Times Editions
An imprint of Marshall Cavendish International (Asia) Private Limited
A member of Times Publishing Limited

Library of Congress Cataloging-in-Publication Data
Gottfried, Ted.
  Slovenia / by Ted Gottfried.
     p. cm. — (Cultures of the world)
  Includes bibliographical references and index.
  ISBN 0-7614-1857-1
  1. Slovenia—Juvenile literature. I. Title. II. Series.
  DR1360.G678 2004
  949.73—dc22   2004022240

Printed in China

7 6 5 4 3 2 1

CONTENTS

Two Slovenian women
enjoy watching the annual
carnival held in Ptuj.

A fountain in Mestni Square in Ljubljana.

INTRODUCTION

SLOVENIA is a picturesque and dynamic nation that has only been in existence since 1991. Before then, it was part of Communist Yugoslavia. Except for the ten-day war that preceded its independence, Slovenia has escaped the violence of such other former Yugoslav states as Bosnia and Croatia. Slovenia's scenic beauty is enriched by village and city architecture bearing the imprint of the Venetian Republic and the Hapsburg Empire, both of which once ruled over its territory. Nestled in the very heart of Europe, between the Adriatic Sea and the Alps, Slovenia is rich in natural resources. It has developed rapidly into a prosperous country and has been a member of the United Nations since May 1992. On March 23, 2003, 86 percent of the Slovenian population voted in favor of Slovenia's joining the European Union, and 66 percent voted in favor of joining NATO. Slovenia's people look to the future, and view nation-building in terms of past successes and attainable goals. This volume, part of the *Cultures of the World* series, introduces a unique nation and people as they emerge into prominence in the 21st century.

GEOGRAPHY

SLOVENIA, where the sun shines an average of 2,000 hours each year, is a land of snow-capped mountains, melodic waterfalls, sprawling forests, tranquil lakes, rolling hills, grassy plains, rambling rivers, spectacular caves, and a smidgeon of seashore with sparkling beaches.

LOCATION

In central Europe, Slovenia nestles like a small, jagged piece of a jigsaw puzzle between Austria (to the north), Croatia (to the south), Italy (to the west), and Hungary (to the east). It covers an area of 7,825 square miles (20,273 square km), slightly smaller than the state of Massachusetts. A shoreline of 29 miles (46.6 km) is on the Adriatic Sea.

The Julian Alps of northwestern Slovenia rise to heights of over 9,000 feet (2,743 m). Mount Triglav, the tallest peak in Slovenia, is 9,397 feet (2,864 m) high, and offers a spectacular view of deep valleys and wide plateaus. These plateaus extend throughout southwestern and southern Slovenia, a limestone region of underground rivers, gorges, and caves. Inland from the southern coast of the country are farmlands, which provide a variety of vegetables and fruits. The eastern part of Slovenia is an area of hills separated by large plains of gravel and clay. Central Slovenia is heavily forested. Woodlands cover almost half of Slovenia. Farmlands—fields, orchards, vineyards, and pastures—are sometimes at risk of being overrun by the forests.

There are many rivers in Slovenia. The 182-mile (292-km) Kolpa River runs along much of the border with Croatia. The interior of the country is irrigated by the Sava and the Drava rivers, which empty into the Danube. The Soca River flows into the Adriatic Sea. Slovenia also has many lakes.

This diverse land of mountains, forests, and seashore experiences a changeable climate.

Opposite: **The snow-capped Julian Alps make a picturesque backdrop to this Alpine village.**

Slovenia experiences the four seasons. Winter is a time for Slovenian children to have fun in the snow.

SEASONS AND CLIMATE

Climates in Slovenia vary in the different regions. The Julian Alps and the valleys in the northwest are very cold in winter and pleasantly mild in summer. Farther west, and along the Adriatic coast, autumn and spring offer many warm, sunny days, and the winters are mild. Eastern Slovenia has very hot summers and very cold winters. In the country as a whole, January is the coldest month, with an average daytime temperature of 28 degrees Fahrenheit (-2 degrees Celsius). In July the average temperature is 70° F (21° C). The average annual precipitation is 31.5 inches (800 mm) in the east, and as much as 118 inches (3,000 mm) in the northwest.

REGIONS

Slovenia is divided geologically into twelve regions. They are Gorenjska, Central Slovenia, Dolenjska, Zasavje, Posavje, Savinjsko, Koroska, Podravje, Pomurje, Goriska, Notranjska, and Primorska.

GORENJSKA This region is dominated by the Julian Alps, an eastern branch of the Italian Alps that extends southeastward almost to central Slovakia. They are a major attraction for foreign skiers, and native Slovenes also flock to the Julian slopes in the winter months. (One out of four Slovenes is an active skier.) The warm alpine lakes of Bled and Bohinj are also in Gorenjska. The region's most popular resort is Vogel, which has ski runs that provide a breathtaking view of the Bohinj Valley. Mount Triglav, the jewel in the crown of the region, is featured on the nation's flag and the national coat of arms. Kranj, a bustling industrial city, is in the center of Gorenjska.

CENTRAL SLOVENIA Central Slovenia includes the central part of the Ljubljana Basin and the hills that surround it. The city of Ljubljana (lee U blee AH nuh), the capital of Slovenia, is located here. The Ljubljanica River flows alongside the city, and the Sava River is nearby. Major European transportation routes crisscross Central Slovenia, and many of them intersect in Ljubljana, the nation's largest business center. Ljubljana's prosperity has spread over the region.

DOLENJSKA Extending south from Ljubljana to the Croatian border and the Kolpa River, Dolenjska is a hilly area of small villages linked by the

Climbers brave the weather to reach the summit of Mount Triglav, Slovenia's highest peak.

9

Ljubljana-Zagreb highway. The region has lush vineyards, and is crisscrossed by wooded valleys and winding streams. It includes the Gorjanci mountains and the cultural subregion of Bela Krajina. Traditional Slovenian music and dances are performed throughout Bela Krajina, and the area is rich in folklore.

ZASAVJE The Zasavje region, about 37.5 miles (60 km) northeast of Ljubljana, is the most polluted area in Slovenia. A coal mining area heavy with soot and smoke, Zasavje has been nicknamed the "Black District." Its major towns of Trbovlje, Zagorje, Savi, and Hrastnik are the most polluted by sulfur dioxide and black smoke. While the mines have become less productive, cement works, chemical factories, and power plants operating without pollution control equipment have continued to poison Zasavje's air. Mountains and valleys characterize the Zasavje landscape, and the deep gorge of the Sava River cuts through the area.

POSAVJE East-southeast of Ljubljana, the Posavje region follows the lower stream of the Sava River to the Croatian border. It is a highly cultivated area of rolling hills, orchards, and vineyards. The Krakoski Gozd oak forest, where the hills even off into flatlands, attracts many campers and hikers. Thermal springs, Slovenia's largest natural health attraction, are near the banks of the Sotla River. A hydroelectric plant at Vrhovo in Posavje harnesses the power of the Sava River. Slovenia's only nuclear power plant is in the Posavje town of Krsko.

The steeple of the Chapter Church in Novo Mesto can be seen from afar. Novo Mesto (New Town) is the main manufacturing, business, and cultural center of Dolenjska.

SAVINJSKO To the north of Posavje lies the Savinjsko region. It contains the watershed of the Savinja River, which runs from the Karavanke Mountains to the Savinja Valley. Hop plantations spread out over the Savinja Valley, while the Zalek Valley has the largest lignite coal mine in Slovenia. Celje, an ancient Roman town, is Slovenia's third largest city.

KOROSKA Farther north is the region of Koroska, which extends to the Austrian border. It encompasses the mountains through which the Drava, Mezica, and Mislinja rivers run. Although there are isolated farms carved out of the forested areas, it is in the valleys that industry has developed. Foremost is the ironworks at Ravne. Most notable is the city of Slovenj Gradec, a cultural center devoted to promoting peace in the world.

PODRAVJE West of Koroska, the region of Podravje offers a varied terrain. It includes the hills of Slovenske Gorice, the forested mountains of Pohorje, and the plains of Drava and Ptuj. Its most scenic attractions may be the large, artificial recreation lakes—Maribor Lake, Ptuj Lake, Ormoz Lake—created by damming the swift-flowing Drava River. Famous for the quality of its white wines, Podravje boasts Slovenia's second largest city, Maribor. The oldest city in Slovenia, Ptuj, is also in Podravje.

POMURJE Located between Austria, Hungary, and Croatia, Pomurje is divided by the Mura River. The most northeast region of Slovenia, it covers a large agricultural plain known as the Slovenian breadbasket. The plain lies between the Goricko hills to the north and the Slovenske Gorice hills to the south. The woodlands of Goricko are famous hunting grounds and were once owned by an Austrian empress. Murska Sobota is Pomurje's major city. However, the castle Grad, its major attraction, is decaying into a ruin.

Pomurge is renowned for the healing qualities of its many hot springs and its mineral waters. Sanitariums are an important factor in the region's economy.

PRIMORSKA In central western Slovenia, the region of Primorska runs south along the Italian border to the Adriatic Sea. Primorska takes in the entire small Slovenian coast, including the port of Koper, the nation's maritime gateway to the world. In addition to a sparkling seaside, there are croplands rich in a variety of vegetables, as well as sun-drenched olive groves. Lipizzaners—the all-white performing horses of the royal Austrian court of the Hapsburgs, who once ruled Slovenia—are sometimes bred here and may be seen prancing along the byways, and even on the beaches.

NOTRANJSKA Between Primorska and Central Slovenia, Notranjska is famous for its systems of underground caves and natural tunnels. The most famous are the Skocjan Caves, which include an underground canyon that stretches for 545 yards (498 m); a section called Paradise, filled with other-worldly stalactites, stalagmites, and water-polished flowstones; a former riverbed called Calvary; and the Great Hall, which is 394 feet (120 m) wide and 98 feet (30 m) high. There are 250 varieties of plants and five types of bats in the caves. Notranjska also has a thriving industry of pig, sheep, and cattle breeding, and heavily forested areas, which have fostered the development of wood processing factories.

GORISKA In the northeastern corner of Slovenia where its borders with Austria and Italy meet, the region of Goriska stretches from the mountain peaks of the Alps to the cave-lands of Notranjska. It contains the watershed of the Soca, Slovenia's most beautiful river. During World War I many devastating battles between Austrian and Italian troops were fought along the banks of the Soca. The award-winning museum in the Goriska city of Kobarid documents them. Goriska's other city, Nova Gorica, is very different from Kobarid. Considered the social center of the region, it features an elaborate entertainment center and casino and draws many tourists.

CITIES

Of the approximately 6,000 settlements in Slovenia, 167 are large enough to be considered cities. As of the 2001 census, 49.2 percent of the Slovenian population lived in these urban centers. As in many developing countries, there is a shift from rural to urban areas, but the movement is slow in Slovenia, with projections indicating that by the year 2015 the urban count will only have risen to 51.6 percent of the Slovenian population.

The blue waters of the Adriatic Sea off the coastal city of Piran is an attraction for both locals and tourists.

LJUBLJANA The most populous city in Slovenia is the capital, Ljubljana, with over a quarter of a million people. Ljubljana is a combination of a bustling urban area, a university town with 35,000 students, and a throwback to the old Europe of baroque churches, fountains, and sculptures. Its thousand-year-old castle features a pentagon-shaped tower that offers a breathtaking view of the city, including the gargoyle-fringed rooftops of the district known as Old Town. Looking out beyond the city, the view includes the Julian Alps and the three peaks of Mount Triglav, the mysterious barje marshlands, the brightly lit cafes lining the banks of the Ljubljanica River, and Tivoli Park, with its recreation center featuring bowling alleys, tennis courts, swimming pools, and a roller-skating rink

Ljubljana began as an outpost of the Roman legions in the first century B.C., and there are still ruins testifying to the Roman occupation. In the 14th century the Hapsburg dynasty of Austria-Hungary took over the city. They built many of the lovely white mansions and churches that are still standing. Napoleon captured the city in 1809 and held it for five years. During that time, by his order, Ljubljana was the capital of what he called the Illyrian Provinces. In 1918, following World War I, the city became part of the newly formed nation of Yugoslavia. It became the capital of Slovenia following the breakaway from Yugoslavia in 1991.

SLOVENJ GRADEC Nestled between the Mount Urslja Gora and the western Pohorje mountain range where the Mislinja and Suhodolnica rivers meet, Slovenj Gradec dates back to 1191. A walled city with a rich crafts tradition, its attractions include a Gallery of Fine Arts, the Koroska Regional Museum, and the Soklic Museum. It has four picturesque churches and has maintained, in its original condition, the house where the composer Hugo Wolf was born, in 1860. Vodriz Castle stands just outside the city.

Wearing the honorable title of the "Peace Messenger City" of the United Nations, Slovenj Gradec holds a yearly Festival of Peace, actively involving the municipal government, the city's schoolchildren and United Nations Educational, Scientific and Cultural Organization (UNESCO). Schoolchildren work on UNESCO peace projects throughout the year. Adult citizens' devotion to the cause of nonviolence and peaceful conflict resolution has made Slovenj Gradec a model for peace activists around the world.

KOPER Behind the district of shipping warehouses that line the harbor, Koper is a city of narrow, cobbled streets and winding back alleys. The town square is surrounded on all four sides by interesting buildings. These include the City Tower, the Cathedral of St. Nazarius, the 12th century Carmine Rotunda, the 15th-century Pretorian Palace, and the Koper Town Hall. South of the square is Shoemakers Street, an avenue of expensive shops. Farther along is Almerigogna Palace, a Venetian gothic structure decorated with Renaissance frescoes. All this is out of sight of the harbor, where cargoes are being loaded, ships are pulling up anchor, and the bustle of commerce is defining Slovenia's major seaport.

Opposite: **Some of the buildings in Old Town Ljubljana are located by the Ljubljanica River. Many of these buildings house museums, cafés, and art galleries today.**

PTUJ Believed to be the oldest city in Slovenia, Ptuj is the cultural center of the district of Podravje. The municipal government has assigned landmark status to the city's many historical buildings and monuments to protect them from the wrecking crews of developers. The castle, the Dominican monastery, the old city hall, and the patrician houses with their intricately carved doors, wrought-iron window grilles, and stone-cut facades are all preserved. Three times a year the residents of Ptuj stage colorful festivals, and costumed revelers dance on the city streets. Every Saturday musicians gather in front of the city hall to serenade newlyweds.

THE HILLS ARE ALIVE . . .

In the eastern part of Slovenia, the Pannonian hills and plains cover more than one-fifth of the country. They make up the nation's main agricultural area with large fields of corn, wheat, and sugar beets in the flatlands and orchards and vineyards on the hillsides. Three-quarters of this land lies less than 984 feet (300 m) above sea level.

Grapevines are planted in autumn in the so-called thermal zone of the Pannonian hills because temperatures are warmer there than in the surrounding areas. With the exception of the red Modra Frankinja wine, the wine made from these grapes is white. There are also springs from which the much-prized Radenska "Three Hearts" mineral water is bottled. Local people mix the mineral water with their wine to create a spritzer.

The sounds of music define the Pannonian fields, where the hardworking tillers of the soil sing or play traditional folk songs on hand-carved instruments—flutes and lutes and unnamed others—at day's end. Along with their knack for dry, understated humor, the music of the Pannonian people defines their gentle spirit. The terrain has instilled in them the easygoing rhythm of dawn-to-dusk labor and twilight-to-sunrise relaxation. They truly go with the flow of the seasons and the always sunny climate.

MARIBOR The second largest city in Slovenia, Maribor stands at the crossroads of traffic routes leading from central Europe. During the last 50 years it has changed from a provincial town of merchants and craftspeople to an economically dynamic city with a major university. Maribor's winter stadium serves as headquarters for women's World Cup slalom competitions. In addition to a varied and historic architecture, Maribor features a national theater where operas are performed, a city park, and an aquarium. Some of the vineyards surrounding Maribor are over 400 years old.

NOVA GORICA Often called the Slovenian Las Vegas, Nova Gorica is a relatively new city—unusual in Slovenia—built after World War II. Situated on the Italian border, Nova Gorica attracts many tourists to its gambling casinos and entertainment houses. Its economic development is based on attracting industry and promoting small businesses, many of which are associated with the tourist trade. Discos abound, and for thrill seekers there are parachuting and hang-gliding facilities. The medieval castle of Rihemberk is nearby.

Maribor is located in northern Slovenia near the Austrian border. The city center has many art galleries and quaint shops selling Slovenian goods. Maribor is famous for its textile and metal industries. The city was also the industrial center of Slovenia until 1991.

HISTORY

EARLY KNOWLEDGE of the area now known as Slovenia has been lost in the mists of history. There is evidence that the legions of the Roman Empire established settlements there but were later driven out by invading Huns, Goths, and Avars.

In the sixth century the invaders were expelled by Slavs from eastern Europe. In A.D. 623 King Samo established a Slovenian kingdom that stretched from Hungary to the Mediterranean Sea. In A.D. 748 the German-ruled Frankish Empire conquered Slovenia, to be succeeded by the Holy Roman Empire in the ninth century. During this period the Slovenian population was converted to the Christianity of the Roman Catholic Church. The Austro-German monarchy, which would evolve into the Austro-Hungarian Hapsburg Empire, took over in the 14th century and ruled Slovenia—with one brief interruption—until 1918.

Left: **Pope Nicholas V crowned Frederick III, the fifth duke of Austria, as Holy Roman Emperor in 1452. For the next 300 years, every Holy Roman Emperor was a Hapsburg.**

Opposite: **Slovenian president Josip Tito welcomes Premier Nikita Krushchev, the Russian premier (1958-1964) of the Soviet Union, on his visit to Yugoslavia in 1963.**

THE HAPSBURGS AND NAPOLEON

Fifteenth-century Slovenia was an agrarian society, where most of the population worked as farmers.

Early Austro-German rule was harsh. The Austro-German rulers made the Slovenian farmers serfs, who neither owned the estates on which they labored nor profited from them. Upper-class Slovenes conformed to German society and were absorbed into the ruling system, but the majority lower classes retained their Slovenian identity. Slovenia's Roman Catholic priests were instrumental in the preservation of Slovenian culture and worked to encourage pride in the Slovenian heritage.

There was a series of peasant uprisings during the 15th and 16th centuries. These were firmly put down. The condition of the Slovenian serfs did not improve until the 18th century, when the Austro-Hungarian Hapsburg empress Maria Theresa and her son Joseph II decreed reforms. Further reforms followed in 1809, when the French armies of Napoleon seized Slovenia.

Napoleon's invasion of Slovenia was key to his effort to block the Hapsburg Empire's access to the Adriatic Sea. Napoleon eventually conquered Slovenia, Dalmatia, and part of Croatia, decreeing them France's Illyrian Provinces, with Ljubljana as the capital. He held this area for five years. During that time the French instituted sweeping reforms in education, law, and in the Slovenian government. When the Hapsburg administrators returned in 1814, these reforms were firmly in place, and they were unable to dislodge them.

KINGDOM OF SERBS, CROATS, AND SLOVENES

In 1848 democratic revolution swept across Europe, giving birth to a desire for freedom among Slovenes. Slowly, a movement for political independence from the Hapsburg Empire began to form. However, a century would go by before that dream would be realized. It would take World War I and

the breakup of the Austro-Hungarian Empire to release Slovenia from Hapsburg rule.

At the end of World War I, in 1918, various areas of what had been the Austro-Hungarian Empire became separate, independent nations. Slovenia became part of the Kingdom of the Serbs, Croats, and Slovenes, ruled by the Serbian Karageorgevic family dynasty. The initial ruler was King Peter I, and when he died after three years on the throne, the crown went to his son, King Alexander I.

The new kingdom was afflicted by high inflation, internal rivalries between Serbs and Croats, and territorial disputes with neighboring countries. In 1929, to avoid chaos, King Alexander imposed a royal dictatorship. That same year he changed the name of the country from the Kingdom of Serbs, Croats, and Slovenes to the kingdom of Yugoslavia. Total chaos was avoided, but internal disruptions cropped up constantly during the next five years. These occurred less often, and were generally less violent, in Slovenia than in other parts of Yugoslavia.

King Alexander I, pictured here with his wife, Princess Marie, changed the country's name to the kingdom of Yugoslavia in 1929.

WORLD WAR II

In 1934 during a diplomatic visit to Marseilles, France, King Alexander was assassinated by Croatian terrorists. His 11-year-old son, Crown Prince Peter, became king. Prince Peter's great-uncle, Prince Paul, husband of Princess Olga of Greece, became the prince regent who actually governed Yugoslavia along with two other regents.

World War II broke out in most of Europe in 1939. By 1941, all but one of Yugoslavia's neighbors had fallen to the Nazis. In March 1941 Prince Paul signed a pact with Germany and her ally Italy. Soon after, on March 27, 1941, Prince Paul was removed in a bloodless palace coup. King Peter II, then 18 years old, was able to legally ascend to the throne.

His reign did not last long. Within a week Germany, Italy, Hungary, and Bulgaria invaded Yugoslavia. The government was forced to surrender, and King Peter had to flee the country. He made his way to London, where he set up a Yugoslav government in exile.

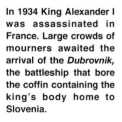

In 1934 King Alexander I was assassinated in France. Large crowds of mourners awaited the arrival of the *Dubrovnik,* the battleship that bore the coffin containing the king's body home to Slovenia.

THE HOLOCAUST LESSON

There are no separate statistics for Slovenia's Jewish population at the start of World War II. Nobody knows how many Slovenian Jews died in the Holocaust, but it is estimated that in 1941, before the start of World War II, there were roughly 70,000 Jews in Yugoslavia. By the end of 1945, approximately 60,000 had been killed by the Nazis. Many Jews were hunted down (*right*), arrested, and sent to concentration camps. Roughly 86 percent of Yugoslavia's Jews perished in the Holocaust. Countless Slovenian Jews were among them.

Jews had migrated to Slovenia in the 13th century. As early as 1277, the walled city of Maribor had a "Jewish street" and a synagogue. There were also Jewish communities in the cities of Ptuj, Celje, Radgona, and Ljubljana. However, in 1496 the emperor Maximilian I of Austria drove all Jews out of Slovenia. In the 19th and early 20th centuries they began drifting back, but it wasn't until the establishment of the Kingdom of Serbs, Croats, and Slovenes that Jews from other parts of the country, where anti-Semitism ran high, migrated in large numbers to Slovenia.

In January 2000 President Milan Kucan of the Republic of Slovenia addressed an international forum on the Holocaust in Stockholm, Sweden. President Kucan ended his speech by offering the hope that "the Holocaust and the genocide against all nations who fell victim to it, as well as its causes and consequences, [would] find their proper place in the schoolbooks of all democratic countries of the world."

and King Peter had to flee the country. He made his way to London, where he set up a Yugoslav government in exile.

Meanwhile, a large part of Slovenia was annexed by Germany, with Italy and Hungary laying claim to the remaining areas. From 1941 through the end of the war in 1945, Slovenian partisan groups fought the occupation from bases in the mountains and from underground caves in their country. Toward the end of that same period, with the help of Soviet tank brigades, Serbian partisans drove the Germans from Belgrade, the capital city of Yugoslavia, and established a Communist government. The leader of the highly organized and extremely effective Communist partisan movement in Yugoslavia was Josip Broz, better known as Tito.

TITO: SAVIOR OR DESPOT?

Josip Broz, the Communist dictator of Yugoslavia better-known as Tito, was born into a peasant family on May 7, 1892, in Kumrovec, Croatia. The seventh of 15 children, he was apprenticed to a locksmith at an early age. In 1910, in Vienna, Josip Broz joined the Social Democratic Party. Drafted into the Austro-Hungarian army in 1913, he fought in World War I, was captured by the Russians, and spent time in a prisoner-of-war camp.

After the war Broz married Pelageja Beloussowa, and in 1920 he joined the Communist Party of Yugoslavia (KPJ). He worked as a union agitator and was sentenced to five years in the penitentiary for his Communist activity. Released in 1934, he went underground and adopted the alias of Tito.

In 1941, when the Nazis and their allies occupied Yugoslavia, Tito organized the Communist partisan resistance movement. In 1943 Tito was wounded in combat and named marshal of Yugoslavia. In 1945, as the war drew to a close, Tito organized a new Yugoslav government and was appointed prime minister.

In November 1945, without putting it to a vote by the people, Tito illegally abolished the monarchy. Yugoslavia, including Slovenia, was now a one-party state—the Federal Republic of Yugoslavia—under the Communist leadership of Prime Minister Tito.

In 1948 Soviet leader Joseph Stalin expelled Tito and Yugoslavia from the world Communist movement after Tito started showing signs of excessive independence. In 1953 Tito was named president as well as prime minister. In 1974 he was named president for life. After 35 years as the dictator of Communist Yugoslavia, Tito died at the age of 88 in Ljubljana, on May 4, 1980.

Domestically, Tito's greatest accomplishment was keeping the lid on the animosity between the Serbs of Bosnia-Herzegovina and the Croats of Croatia, whose violent feuding preceding World War I was heightened by pro- and anti-Nazi actions during World War II, and would break into full-scale war during the years following Tito's death.

UNDER COMMUNIST RULE

On November 29, 1945, the Federal Republic of Yugoslavia was formed, with Tito at its head. King Peter II had not abdicated, but he had no armies to enforce any effort to reclaim his throne. Tito would rule Yugoslavia for the next 35 years. However, because he refused to follow the Communist Party line dictated by Moscow, Yugoslavia's relations with the United States and other democratic nations were better than those of any other Communist country.

During Tito's regime there was tenfold growth in industrial output between pre-World War II and 1970. Between 1947 and 1980 farm production expanded, and exports of wood products from forests increased. As part of Tito's power grid, many hydroelectric plants were built to harness river power. Increased tourism contributed to the economy. Under Tito the entire population of Yugoslavia was covered by health insurance.

The bubble burst in 1979. A worldwide oil crisis caused a lasting shock to the Yugoslav industrial development strategy when the price of fuel to run the country's factories skyrocketed. Between 1975 and 1980 inflation had reached an annual rate of 50 percent. By the time Tito died in 1980, his Communist policies were already becoming unpopular with the Yugoslav people.

Marshal Tito inspects Yugoslav troops in the small border town of Capodistria.

THE INDEPENDENCE MOVEMENT

Following Tito's death, the Communist system in Yugoslavia began to crumble. In 1982 the Krajgher Commission, assigned to come up with recommendations for dealing with the collapsing economy, released plans for a long-term economic stabilization program. Among their recommendations was a wage austerity program that reduced workers' salaries. The Yugoslav Federal Assembly passed only 8 of the 25 Krajgher Commission proposals.

Attempts by the Communist government to shift capital from rich areas to poor areas aroused particular resentment in Slovenia. Feelings ran high that Slovenes should not have to pay forever for underdeveloped regions such as Macedonia, Kosovo, Montenegro, and Bosnia, where the people had not developed profitable industries.

In 1987 a small but influential group of intellectuals called for Slovenia to replace the Communist system with a democratic system, to establish a free-market economy while maintaining public-welfare policies, and to declare independence from Yugoslavia. The proposal caught on with the Slovenian people, and in May 1989 there was a large rally in Ljubljana to support it. By November political parties—the Democratic Alliance of Slovenia, the Social Democrat Alliance of Slovenia, the Slovene Christian Democrats, the Farmer's Alliance, the Greens of Slovenia, and others— had formed and united into the Democratic Opposition of Slovenia (DEMOS). DEMOS won control of the Slovenian parliament in the April 1990 election. Later that year a national vote on independence for Slovenia was held. An unusually large turnout resulted in 88.2 percent in favor of independence. On June 25, 1991, the Slovene Parliament enacted the Declaration of Independence of the Republic of Slovenia, severing the nation from Yugoslavia.

THE 10-DAY WAR

The Yugoslav government opposed allowing Slovenia to secede. The Yugoslav army (YNA) occupied Slovenia's border crossings, cutting the country off from the outside while maintaining Yugoslav sovereignty over it. Plans were under way to replace the rebellious government of Slovenia. Slovenia responded.

The government organized local territorial defense forces. Police units from various cities were organized. YNA units were blocked from areas they tried to occupy. They were attacked by local militia and police. Large numbers of Slovenian citizens not only resisted the YNA but fought pitched battles with them. After two days, with the Slovenian resistance taking its toll, the YNA threatened retaliatory measures against the civilian population.

Throughout most of Europe, public opinion sided with Slovenia. The European Community sent three diplomats to Zagreb, Yugoslavia to try to arrange a ceasefire. As the conflict heated up, a delegation headed by Yugoslav Federal prime minister Ante Markovic arrived in Zagreb. By then, the YNA had effectively been defeated in Slovenia. Yugoslavia had no choice but to agree to a ceasefire. The armistice decreed that Slovenia would retain control over its territory, including its borders; that trapped YNA units would be allowed to move out; that all prisoners of war on both sides would be released; and that for three months Slovenia would refrain from any further measures designed to finalize its independence. The ten-day war was over.

Two soldiers from the Slovenian Defense Forces guard their tank, which was hit by an anti-tank missile. Fighting between the Yugoslav army and Slovenes broke out in 1991 following Slovenia's independence from Yugoslavia.

In 2004 representatives of the seven new NATO member countries attend a ceremony at the White House in Washington, DC. The ceremony was held to welcome them to NATO. U.S. President George W. Bush *(extreme right)* gives a welcome address as the seven prime ministers, including Prime Minister Anton Rop of Slovenia *(second from left)*, look on.

SLOVENIAN NATIONHOOD

By October 8, 1991, the three-month cooling-off period had passed, the Yugoslav nation was breaking up, and Slovenia began efforts to secure recognition from other nations as an independent state. In January the following year the European Community recognized Slovenia. Recognition by the United States followed in April. In May, Slovenia was accepted into the United Nations, and then admitted to the Council of Europe.

Following independence, the DEMOS ruling coalition began to unravel. There were heated debates between socialist-leaning liberals and strict Catholic conservatives regarding the wording of the new constitution and the privatization of property that had been held publicly under the Communist regime. Nevertheless, agreement was reached and by the end of 1991, a democratic constitution had been adopted.

In December 1992 elections were held and DEMOS was defeated, with the Liberal Democrat Party (LDS) winning enough votes (23 percent) to form a centrist coalition government. This included the Christian Democrats and two center-left socialist democratic parties. The practical and nonideological bills passed by the coalition halted the downward slide in wages, established rules for privatization, rehabilitated banks, and established rules for elections. These stabilized the country and established its soundness among other nations.

Throughout the 1990s, as the other former territories of Yugoslavia were engaged in fierce civil war among Serbs, Croats, and Bosnians, Slovenia remained peaceful. The Slovenes focused on building a free-market economy, improving the nation's infrastructure, attracting foreign investment, perfecting a national health system, reducing unemployment, successfully reducing inflation, and improving agricultural production. These efforts were ongoing as the 21st century began, and in December 2002 an International Monetary Fund (IMF) report concluded that the Slovenian economy showed "considerable resilience" compared to a "weakening of the economic environment in the European Union (EU)."

At the start of 2004 Slovenia stood out among former Communist states as a successful model for the transition to a democratic society.

In 1999 members of the UN Security Council, including Slovenia, voted to adopt a resolution on the Kosovo peace plan. Slovenia has held the Presidency of the UN Security Council twice—in 1998 and 1999.

GOVERNMENT

SLOVENIA IS A democratic republic with a parliamentary system. The nation's authority is shared by executive, legislative, and judicial branches in an arrangement similar to the balance of powers in the federal government of the United States. A president and a prime minister share the duties of heading the government.

Since declaring its independence in 1991 Slovenia has built a stable democratic political system—holding free elections, instituting a free press, and maintaining a positive record on human rights issues. The most prosperous republic of the former Yugoslavia, Slovenia maintains close ties with the West.

THE EXECUTIVE

The president is elected for a five-year term by direct vote of the Slovenian people. He may be reelected for a second consecutive five-year term, but not a third consecutive term. After a term out of office, however, he is eligible to serve again. As head of state, the president represents Slovenia in its dealing with other world leaders, and is commander in chief of the nation's military forces.

The prime minister is nominated by the party that received the most votes in a parliamentary election and is appointed to office by the president. He has authority over the 17-member cabinet and the 58 government administrative units. He reports on government decisions and actions to the National Assembly, and is responsible to it.

Above: **In December 2002 Janez Drnovsek was sworn in as Slovenia's third president.**

Opposite: **The Slovenian flag flies high on a building located at Congress Square in Ljubljana.**

THE LEGISLATIVE

Slovenia's National Assembly (Drzavni Zbor), or parliament, has 90 members who serve 4-year terms. Of these, 40 are directly elected by the people, and 50 are seated on a proportional basis to represent such specific groups as labor unions, farming interests, national minorities, industry groups, and other professional, regional, social, and economic interests.

There is also a 40-member National Council, which is elected every five years. Its role is strictly advisory. It can propose laws to the National Assembly or ask that body to reconsider laws it has passed, but it cannot itself enact legislation.

POLITICAL PARTIES

As of 2004, there were nine political parties represented in Slovenia's National Assembly. Usually these parties form themselves into left, right, or center coalitions to enact legislation.

Party Name	Abbreviation
Democratic Party	DS
Democratic Union	DU
Movement For a Democratic Slovakia	HZDS
Christian Democratic Movement	KDH
Slovak Democratic Coalition	SDK
Party of the Democratic Left	SDL
Hungarian Coalition	SMK
Slovak National Party	SNS
Party of Civil Understanding	SOP

STABILITY

Despite a sizable mixture of political parties, some devoted to single issues, Slovenia has had a remarkably stable government since breaking away from Yugoslavia in 1991. Milan Kucan, who led the country to independence, was its first president and served two terms. Kucan could not immediately run for a third term because of the constitutional provision forbidding it. He was followed by Janez Drnovsek, who was himself elected prime minister in 1992, and won a second term in 1996. Prime Minister Anton Rop was previously finance minister and, like President Drnovsek, a member of the parliamentary majority Liberal Democrat Party.

Prime Minister Anton Rop *(left)* **meets Pope John Paul II** *(right)* **during a visit to the Vatican in May 2004. Anton Rop served as Slovenia's minister of finance before being elected prime minister in December 2002.**

THE FATHER OF HIS COUNTRY

Milan Kucan (*left*), the first president of the independent Republic of Slovenia, was born January 14, 1941, in the village of Prekmurje. Three months later, on April 17, 1941, the Nazis invaded Yugoslavia and occupied Slovenia. Milan's father, a schoolteacher, became an officer in the Slovenian resistance movement against the Nazis, and was killed fighting them.

Although Slovenia was overwhelmingly Catholic, Kucan was raised a Protestant. He attended primary and secondary school in Mursksa Sobota, then went to the University of Ljubljana, graduating in 1964 with a degree in law. He joined the Youth Association of the Yugoslav Republic of Slovenia in 1964 and served as president of the organization in 1968 and 1969. He became a member of the Central Council of the League of Communists of the Republic of Slovenia in 1969 and served through 1973. During this time he helped to prepare the constitutional amendments that brought about decentralization in the Yugoslav federation ruled by Tito.

In 1978 Kucan became president of the Slovene Assembly. Following Marshal Tito's death in 1980, he worked to improve ethnic relations among the diverse groups in Yugoslavia and to have the Communist Party cede more political power to the people. In 1986 Kucan became president of the League of Communists of Slovenia (ZKS) and pushed through measures to reform the organization. Under his leadership the ZKS initiated a multiparty system that brought democracy to Slovenia. Although still a Communist, in 1986 he insisted that the people must have a genuine political voice in government, a voice not limited by party domination. "The freedoms of an individual," he proclaimed in a July 1986 speech that was understood as a challenge to party authority, "are limited solely by the boundaries of equal rights and the freedoms of others."

Although still part of Yugoslavia, Slovenia held its first multiparty elections in 1990, and Kucan became president. He presided over the declaration of Slovenian independence from Yugoslavia and over the 10-day war that ensued. Following the establishment of the independent Republic of Slovenia in 1992, former Communist Kucan, running as an independent candidate with no party affiliation, was elected the new country's first president. He was reelected as an independent in 1997, winning 55.54 percent of the votes against seven opponents.

As president, Kucan achieved a wide consensus among Slovenia's rival political parties. He is credited with rebuilding his country economically and with leading it back into democracy. Although Kucan is out of office, his popularity is so great that there is already a drive for him to run for president at the end of Janez Drnovsek's term in 2007, when he will once again be eligible. Whether he makes the race or not, and whether it is successful or not, Milan Kucan will continue to be regarded as the father of the independent Republic of Slovenia.

THE JUDICIAL SYSTEM

There are 182 administrative divisions, called municipalities, in Slovenia. Of these, 11 are considered urban municipalities, or cities, while the others are towns, villages, or rural areas. All have local self-government with elected officials. All are subject to judicial authority by district and regional courts. Their judgments may be upheld or overruled by appeals courts, or by the Supreme Court of the Republic of Slovenia.

Criminal cases are brought by the local office of the state prosecutor of Slovenia. An ombudsman for human rights and fundamental freedoms, elected by the National Assembly for a period of six years, may intervene in cases in which rights under the Slovenian constitution are called into question. Such cases go before judges of the Constitutional Court, who have the expertise to decide on constitutional issues.

The municipality of Gorenjska, located in the Julian Alps, is one of 11 urban municipalities.

35

ECONOMY

SINCE DECLARING its independence, Slovenia successfully made the transition from Communism to capitalism, allowing the Slovenian people to enjoy a quality of life that in many respects exceeds the average for other European countries. The nation established and encouraged private rather than public ownership, increased and stabilized the value of its currency, reined in inflation, halted rising unemployment, and modernized its taxation system. Despite the economic slowdown in Europe in 2001–2002, Slovenia maintained a 3 percent annual growth rate. Slovenia's gross domestic product (GDP) has grown steadily, with services accounting for the highest percentage (60.5 percent), followed by industry (36.3 percent) and agriculture (3.2 percent).

Left: **A foundry worker In a factory in Aealec pours molten metal to make bells.**

Opposite: **Slovenes wait at a bus stop in downtown Ljubljana.**

SERVICES

Those enterprises accounting for the major part of the Slovenia's GDP include so many diverse activities that they might as well be classified as nonindustrial, nonagricultural endeavors rather than services. Among them are telecommunication companies; legal, architectural, and engineering firms; social services such as health care, wholesaling, retailing, and franchising enterprises; schools, colleges, and universities; accounting and advertising businesses; engineering and construction enterprises; railway and trucking firms; utility companies; travel and tourism services; and many others. One such service is the Bank Austria Creditanstalt Slovenija. This bank is part of an extensive international banking network that offers financial and consulting services to Slovenian companies. It is one of an increasing number of foreign firms offering

Right: **The Slovenia Telecom building is located in Ljubljana. In 2002 Slovenia had more than 1 million telephone main lines in use and about 1.7 million cellular phone subscribers.**

Opposite: **A boat takes tourists across Lake Bled to visit the island located in the center of the lake.**

domestic services to Slovenians. The nuclear power station at Krsko, on the Slovenian side of the border with Croatia, is half-owned by Croatia and produces 39 percent of Slovenia's electricity. Also, many Slovenian-owned enterprises classified as services are financed by foreign investment. As of 2002, foreign direct investment increased to over 2 percent of Slovenia's GDP.

Tourism is a major Slovenian service industry. Each year 1.2 million tourists might visit from other countries. Most are from Italy, Germany, and Austria, with an increasing number both from other European countries and the United States. The ski slopes are a main attraction, as are the more than 4,347 miles (7,000 km) of marked mountain trails for hiking and climbing. Some tourists come for the health benefits of the thermal mineral waters of Slovenia's 15 natural spas. Others are attracted by the 12.5 miles (20 km) of underground passages of the Postojna Caves with their otherworldly stalagmites and stalactites. The Bled and Bohinj lakes in the shadows of the Alps; the Adriatic seacoast; and the Lipica stud farms where the royal Lipizzaner horses are bred, are also major attractions. Busing, housing, feeding and arranging itineraries for foreign and domestic tourists provides work for many Slovenes.

INDUSTRY

Major industries in Slovenia produce electrical equipment, processed foods, textiles, paper products, chemicals, and wood products. Coal is the most abundant natural resource. There are also facilities to mine lead, zinc, mercury, uranium, and silver, as well as modest amounts of natural gas and petroleum.

There are more than 144,000 companies registered in Slovenia. Because of the small size of Slovenia's own domestic market, most of these enterprises are involved in manufacturing or shipping for export to other countries. The main exports are machinery and transport equipment, chemicals, footwear, and household goods. In 1999 the value of Slovenian exports exceeded $8.5 billion. That figure grew to $10.3 billion in 2002, a 5.9 percent increase over the previous year.

Initially, Slovenia exported to targeted traditional trading partners such as Germany, Italy, Austria, and France. Exports then expanded slowly to other members of the European Union. Exports to the United States increased.

Recently, there has been a sizable increase in Slovenian exports to the former countries of Yugoslavia: Bosnia, Croatia, Serbia & Montenegro, and Macedonia. In the first 11 months of 2002, goods sold to these countries jumped by 11.6 percent over the same period in 2001. These markets constituted 18 percent of the total of Slovenian exports during that period.

TRANSPORTATION

There are 16 airports in Slovenia, of which six have paved runways. Ljubljana, Maribor, and Portoro are the three international airports. Flights from Ljubljana regularly connect with all major European airports. Adria Airways (*left*) is the Slovenian national carrier.

Slovenian railways cover 746 miles (1,201 km) and crisscross the country to reach all major Slovenian cities. Offshoots of the four main lines from Ljubljana in the center of Slovenia split off at various points to cover the nation. At key transfer points they connect with each other. There are links to all the major railways of Europe. In addition to transporting passengers, Slovenia's locomotives pull trains carrying 14.5 million tons of freight per year.

The road network of Slovenia extends over 12,530 miles (20,177 km), providing access to all but the most remote regions of the country. All but is 13 miles of the roads are paved, including 265 miles (427 km) of expressways. Road-building projects are presently under way to build an east-west expressway from Sentilj to Koper and a north-south highway from the Karavanke Tunnel on the Austrian border to Obrecje on the Croatian border. Entry to Slovenia from the Adriatic Sea is through the ports of Koper, Izola, and Piran.

A large farm near Kranjska Gora grows crops such as hops and wheat for export and domestic consumption.

AGRICULTURE

Farm and ranch families have a hard life in Slovenia. With some exceptions, the climate and terrain are not hospitable to crops and do not make for good grazing lands. Much of the country is cold and humid. In the southwestern and northeastern regions, where temperatures soar, there is serious drought during the summer months.

Only 11.8 percent of the land of Slovenia is arable. Raising animals for meat is the most productive sector of Slovenian agriculture. Field crops are cultivated mainly for forage by cattle, but also for sheep, goats, and pigs. The next most successful use of land is for orchards and vineyards. Fruit grows on 4 percent of all agricultural land and constitutes between 3 percent and 5 percent of agricultural production. Apples are the main fruit crop, followed by pears, peaches, and cherries. The fruit can be used for wine, and roughly 35 percent of Slovenian farms supplement their income by bottling and selling wine. A small percentage of land is hospitable to barley, corn, potato, soybean, wheat, and sugar beet production.

Slightly more than 2 percent of the Slovenian population are involved in farming or ranching. There are few agribusinesses, and small family farms are the rule. The average size of a Slovenian farm is 8 acres (3.2 hectares). Overgrowing of farmland by Slovenian forests is a serious problem. According to the Slovenian Ministry of Agriculture, Forestry, and Food, there has been an increase in abandoned farms and overgrown farmlands. The low social status of farmers, and their failure to organize into guilds and unions, have persuaded many of their children to reject farm life. The average age of a farm owner in Slovenia today is 58 years. This, according to the ministry, could create future problems in meeting the nation's produce needs.

Despite the difficulties, however, and in part due to the small size of Slovenia's population, there is presently a surplus of Slovenian-grown food, resulting in a growing export trade.

A woman inspects the grapevines in a vineyard to ensure that the grapes are ready for harvesting.

THE CENTRAL BANK

On June 25, 1991, the National Assembly of the Republic of Slovenia passed the Law on the Bank of Slovenia, creating a central bank. The Bank of Slovenia is the supervisor of the Slovenian banking system. It is a nongovernmental, independent institution that reports to the National Assembly every six months.

The bank's primary tasks are to issue national currency, to maintain its stability, and to assure its availability for payments within the country and to foreign countries. It is the banker of the government, and conducts no business with corporations or individuals. It may participate in arranging loans for the Slovenian government from foreign countries, but is not allowed to obtain loans abroad for itself, or for other persons or institutions. The bank's governor and a nine-member governing board make all decisions for the Bank of Slovenia.

THE CHAMBER OF COMMERCE

The Chamber of Commerce and Industry of Slovenia began in 1850 as the Chamber of Trades and Industry of Kranjsko. Today it has a membership of 53,000 Slovenian businesses and manufacturers.

The organization provides numerous consulting services and conducts more than 300 classes for over 6,000 participants a year. It annually organizes over 40 business conferences, participates in more than 50 trade fairs, and issues and distributes more than 100,000 documents.

Besides providing information, the chamber maintains a Court of Honor to promote best practices and high principles of business ethics and professional morals; and oversees a Permanent Court of Arbitration to mediate and decide domestic and international disputes in cases voluntarily submitted to its jurisdiction.

MONEY, MONEY, MONEY!

The Bank of Slovenia (*left*) issues the currency of Slovenia in various denominations of bills and coins. According to economic conditions, government needs, and usage, it releases various amounts of different denominations when, in its judgment, it is necessary to do so. The Republic of Slovenia monetary unit is the *tolar* (TOH-lar). Just as the dollar in the United States is made up of 100 cents, the Slovenian tolar subdivides into 100 *stotins* (stoh-TINS).

It follows that larger denominations of the tolar are in more general use, particularly by foreign visitors, than the one tolar coin. There are presently 9 denominations of banknotes and 9 coin values in circulation in Slovenia. The bills are worth, respectively, 10, 20, 50, 100, 200, 500, 1,000, 5,000, and 10,000 tolars. The coins are issued in denominations of 10, 20, and 50 stotins, and 1, 2, 5, 10, 20, and 50 tolars.

Slovenian banknotes honor the heroes of the nation's past. Significantly, these heroes were artists, writers, and other creative personalities. The largest banknote (10,000 tolars) portrays early 20th century author Ivan Cankar. Painter Ivana Kobilca's image is on the 5,000-tolar bill, while the face of 19th-century Slovenian poet France Preseren is on the 1,000-tolar note. The 500-tolar bill honors 19th-century architect Joze Plecnik; the 200-tolar note, 16th-century composer Iacobus Gallus; and the 100-tolar denomination, painter Rihard Jakopic. Mathematician Jurij Vega, historian Janez Vajkard Valvasor, and Primoz Trubar (the writer of the first book in the Slovenian language) are honored respectively on the 50- , 20- , and 10-tolar banknotes.

ENVIRONMENT

DIFFERENT KINDS OF pollution present ongoing problems in Slovenia. Outdated sewage and waste disposal equipment, industry carelessness, and carelessness by people themselves all contribute to these problems. In most rural areas, farms are interspersed with forests. Both foresters and farmers live off the land, and that causes problems. One such problem is the overgrowth of farmlands due to the encouragement of forest growth for profit. Another is the exploitation of the woodlands' trees by those who own them, those who work for the owners, and those who roam the forests.

INTERNATIONAL AGREEMENTS

If the environmental situation appears grim for Slovenia, it should be pointed out that it is no worse than that of many other developing European nations. Safeguarding the environment is a worldwide problem. Nevertheless, Slovenia is an active participant in most of the international agreements forged to protect and improve the environment. Along with Croatia and Italy, Slovenia is a member of the Trilateral Commission for Protection of the Adriatic Sea. Slovenia participates in the United Nations Environment Program, as well as the Fourth Framework Program of the European Union on environment. Among the international agreements to protect the environment that Slovenia has signed are the Energy Charter Treaty, the Protocol on Mountain Forests, the Protocol on Hillside Farming, the Protocol on Nature Protection and Landscape Management, the Convention on the Protection of the Alps, the Convention on Nuclear Safety, the Control of Transboundary Movements of Hazardous Wastes Convention, and many others. The Slovenian nation and its people value their environment and have the will to preserve it. Their determination will surely transform that will into the necessary action.

Opposite: **The fissured ground made of soft limestone forms part of the landscape at the Triglav Lakes valley in Triglav National Park.**

47

FORESTS

Forests cover 55 percent of the land area of Slovenia, and 70 percent of the woodlands are privately owned. Small farmers who own patches of woodlands, or whose fields abut public woodlands, have traditionally chopped the trees into logs for construction and firewood. They have made furniture and built houses from the products of neighboring woodlands—whether they owned them or not. They have heated their houses and barns with split logs and sold the leftovers to others. Many of them have cleared forests and used the land for grazing cattle. They have gathered fruit, nuts, berries, herbs, and mushrooms for their tables, and

Many forests in Slovenia have been cut down to make way for farms.

regularly peddled the excess for income. Over the years this nut-and-berry income has become quite important for rural dwellers. The practice has brought locals into conflict with Romany, or gypsy, groups who roam the woodlands and who also gather its edibles. Communities have tried to assign settlement locations for the Roma where their gathering activities will not interfere with local practices, but the efforts have not been too successful.

The Forest Development Program of Slovenia (FDPS) is charged with managing the nation's woodlands on the basis of ecologically sound land-use plans. It acts on the basis of the Helsinki Resolutions signed at the Ministerial Conference on the Protection of Forests in Europe in 1993. The Slovenian Forest Service monitors the forests and prepares growth and clearing plans for specific forest areas; assists the owners in selecting trees to be chopped down; conducts education and training sessions for foresters, forest owners, and forest workers; and consults with environmental groups, hunting clubs, hiking clubs, and concerned rural area representatives. Care is taken to see that specific kinds of trees are protected and that a balance is maintained among the species of trees and other plant growth of an area. Wildlife, their feeding habits and population growth, are also taken into consideration.

All forest owners, no matter how small their property, are required to manage their woodlands in accordance with the FDPS guidelines. They are entitled to cofinancing of protection measures and related costs. Where immediate threats to the ecology determine the method of forest management, the support the owner gets from the government may be increased by 10 to 20 percent.

The ibex is protected by Slovenian law because of its decreasing number. This means that it is illegal for people to hunt and kill these animals.

The hilly terrain on which most Slovenian farms stand and problems of irrigation and soil pollution also threaten the future of agriculture in Slovenia.

FARMS

In the developed nations of the world, small farms are becoming a thing of the past. Slovenia, up-to-date in other respects, has not caught up when it comes to agriculture. The output of the average Slovenian farm of 8 acres (3.2 hectares), a quarter the size of the average farm in the European Union, is simply too small to compete on the world market.

The government and the Slovenian Chamber of Agriculture and Forestry are taking measures to deal with the threat. A National Irrigation Program has been instituted to both fight drought and counter periodic flooding. Water from the Drava and Mura rivers is being redirected from alpine regions during dry months to hillside farms. Ninety-one reservoirs have been created in water-shy areas. There has been extensive drilling for groundwater.

Some of this groundwater has been found to contain alarming nitrate concentrations. Such pollutants can be introduced into the vegetables people eat and the forage grass of animals that are butchered for meat. The government has set up a critical warning system to identify and eliminate dangerous substances in soil and produce. A decree that limits the amount of fertilizer and heavy metals introduced into soils is in effect. It also limits the use of sewage sludge and manure in organic agriculture.

PROTECTING THE CAVES

Sewage and other waste products are also an ongoing threat to the famous 25-mile (40-km) stretch of 522 caves in Slovenia. Once pollution enters the waters of the caves it disappears extremely quickly underground and enters the groundwater, which spreads it throughout the underground labyrinth. This threatens the very existence of the creatures that inhabit the caves. Whole species have been lost due to water pollution.

This pollution leaks into cave waters from waste dumps, bathroom wastewater, industrial oil spills, gasoline leaks from cars, and overfertilized soil on nearby farms. Illegal dumping of waste (including both industrial and domestic waste) into cave shafts is also a cause of the pollution.

Not just the caves are at risk. The amount of waste generated in Slovenia is increasing. Most of the nation's landfills will be filled up in five years. Waste products from industrial production are particularly hazardous. While some of these are deposited in small landfills and storage facilities inside the properties of the companies that generate them, this is only a temporary solution. The government has taken action that calls for chemical analysis of waste and decreed that only processed waste material may be disposed of at rubbish dumps. It has also set up strict conditions for creating new, heavily lined dumps to ensure that liquids don't leak into the soil and pollute underground water sources. The government is allocating additional funding for waste disposal, but it continues to be a major problem for Slovenia.

The Skocjan Caves were made a UNESCO World Heritage Site in 1996. Tourists and scientists from around the world come to study the limestone formations in these caves.

AIR, RIVERS, AND SEA

The good news is that the air quality of Slovenia has improved over recent years. Awareness of the problem has grown, extending even to the children, with 60 schools using classroom materials developed for all grade levels to receive and analyze data on air pollution. The bad news is that Slovenia's air monitoring network still needs to be modernized. It has to be adjusted to deal with new pollution types, particularly those chemical pollutants most recently introduced by industry.

In those areas where industry has developed in Slovenia, the terrain aggravates the effects of air pollution. Typical is the northern region of Koroska, where factory production has mushroomed in already populated valleys. Air pollution from smokestacks is held in these valleys by the surrounding mountains like water in a basin. Respiratory ailments prevail,

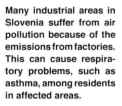

Many industrial areas in Slovenia suffer from air pollution because of the emissions from factories. This can cause respiratory problems, such as asthma, among residents in affected areas.

and the forest system of the valleys is being threatened by acid rain. The Zasavje coal mining region known as the Black District, with its lack of adequate smoke suppression equipment, also suffers greatly from industrial air pollution. Even the Adriatic seaport of Koper is beset by air pollution, as well as other pollution problems. The problems originate with the metallurgical and chemical plants in the area. Coastal waters are contaminated with heavy metals and toxic chemicals. Swimming at area beaches is unsafe. A large wastewater project in the coastal area of Slovenia is planned, but has not yet begun.

In general the waters—lakes, rivers, and ocean—of Slovenia are considered a natural resource and the property of the Republic of Slovenia. They are supposed to be protected by the country's Environmental Protection Act. Nevertheless, industry, farmers, and the general population all contribute to water pollution. Seepage, dumping, and littering are all too prevalent. Treatment of factory and municipal wastewaters is not efficient. The quality of the water in Slovenia's rivers, lakes, and ocean is generally unsatisfactory.

Soca trout live upstream in the clean waters of the Soca River, which has its source in the Julian Alps. The Soca River drains into the Adriatic Sea and supports a variety of wildlife along its course. They are in danger when the river is polluted with toxic waste from farms and factories.

SLOVENES

The 2002 Slovenian census reported a population of approximately 1,964,000 people. Of these, about 83 percent are ethnic Slovenes. There are two communities of Italians and Hungarians who are considered native-born Slovenians with rights protected by the constitution. There are also Romany (Gypsy) communities in Slovenia, with special rights determined by law. Smaller ethnic groups in Slovenia include Croats, Serbs, Bosnians, Macedonians, Montenegrins, and Albanians. Between 250,000 and 400,000 ethnic Slovenes live and work in Italy, Austria, Hungary, and some other European Union countries.

Left: **About 15 percent of Slovenes are over the age of 65.**

Opposite: **Slovenian schoolchildren wave and smile for the camera.**

Slovenian women tend to outlive Slovenian men. The life expectancy for a Slovenian woman is about 80 years.

FACTS AND FIGURES

In Slovenia, the highest 10 percent of the population earns 23 percent of the national income, while the lowest 10 percent earns only 3.9 percent. Nevertheless, even with Slovenia's high unemployment rate of between 11 and 12 percent, no family lives in complete poverty. This may be due to the fact that many low-income Slovenians live off the land in rural areas. They are included in the active Slovenian labor force of 857,400 people.

Approximately half the Slovenian people live in rural areas and half in cities. The population density for the nation is much lower than in most other European countries. The 2003 estimated birth rate of the Slovenian population is 9.23 per 1,000 people. The estimated death rate is 10.15 per 1,000. Because the death rate is greater than the birth rate, it is projected that by the year 2015 the population of Slovenia will decrease by 0.2 percent.

Seventy percent of the population is between 15 and 64 years old. Young people under the age of 14 constitute 15.3 percent of the population, while 14.7 percent is over 65. The average age is 38.6 years.

WOMEN

On average, the women of Slovenia are older than the men. Their median age is 40.2 years as compared with 37.1 years for males. They also live longer than men, with an average life expectancy of 79.5 years compared with the male average life expectancy of 71.6 years.

There are 106 women for every 100 men in Slovenia. The difference may seem slight, but there is a perception among many Slovenian women that there is a shortage of marriageable males in their native country. This has led many Slovenian women to seek husbands abroad, using both the Internet and mail-order bride services to advertise their availability.

Another reason for dissatisfaction may be that in Slovenia the average income for women who work is less than two-thirds of what men earn ($21,338 annually for men as compared with an average of only $13,152 for women). Females and males acquire roughly the same education and have the same literacy rate (an impressive 100 percent compared to 97 percent for the United States), but it does not translate into workplace salaries. This may be because of the distribution of the female workforce. Only 28 percent of female workers are employed in industry, where the better paying jobs are, while 46 percent of male workers have industry jobs. The figures are reversed when it comes to the lower paying service sector. Sixty-one percent of working females are in the service industry while only 42 percent of men are so employed. The discrepancy also prevails in government, where women hold only 12.2 percent of the seats in parliament.

Some Slovenian women choose to manage both family and career as many other women in Europe do.

THE NATIONAL CHARACTER

The Slovenian persona is deep and difficult to define. Marjan Senjur, the Slovenian ambassador to the United Kingdom, has called it "a unique temperament that is a combination of Mediterranean and Central European." On the other hand, several surveys having shown that "xenophobia, a fear of strangers, is deeply ingrained into the Slovenian national character." One poll conducted in Slovenia found 55.6 percent of those who responded believed that refugees who have fled to Slovenia "should not be allowed freedom of movement." At the same time, the Urad za Intervencije (Office of Intervention), a nongovernmental organization,

Slovenes are said to be wary of strangers or foreigners.

was formed in Ljubljana to help refugees. To raise money for them, a charity soccer match between refugees and sympathetic Slovenian journalists was organized under the slogan Fighting Xenophobia with a Ball.

Sadly, for many survivors of people who have taken their own lives, it is suicide that typifies the Slovenian national character. The nation's annual suicide rate is about 30 per 100,000 inhabitants. Some 600 Slovenians kill themselves annually. Considering the small size of the population, this represents a huge problem. It places Slovenia sixth among all the countries of the world in suicides per 100,000 people.

Slovenian suicide rates are increasing. They are increasing at an even greater rate among children. There is fear of a return to the suicide rates of the 1960s, when Slovenia led the world in suicides by young people. Back then, the suicides in Ljubljana of six young people from prominent families closely following one another prompted rumors of a suicide club in the city. The rumors were never confirmed.

The stigma attached to suicide is beginning to lift, as various agencies, such as the Slovenian Association for Suicide Prevention, attempt to create a national strategy for suicide prevention. The Norwegian National Plan for Suicide Prevention is being used as a model for what Slovenia can do to help those citizens who suffer from neuroses and psychoses that may lead to suicide.

Suicide is attempted by women more often than men in Slovenia. However, more men commit suicide successfully than women. It is believed that as many as one-third of suicides among both men and women are related to alcoholism.

An increasing number of incidents of suicide among youths is a cause for concern in Slovenia, which has a history of high suicide rates.

Two Slovenes drinking beer at a café. Drinking alcohol is popular among adults in Slovenia.

ALCOHOLISM

Like suicide, alcoholism is traditionally regarded as a matter of shame rather than a mental health problem by many Slovenians. However, with Slovenia now at the top of the list of worldwide alcohol consumption per unit of population, that may be changing. The government, estimating that every fifth man and every 25th woman in Slovenia is an alcoholic (173,000 alcoholics out of a total population of 2 million), is taking action aimed at making liquor harder to get.

On January 28, 2003, the Slovenian legislature passed an antialcohol bill by a vote of 37 to 12. Tone Partljic, one of the Liberal Democrat sponsors of the bill and a former alcoholic, testifies that "alcoholism is a disease that many people want to hide." He believes the new law "will help people come to terms with their drinking problems." It bars the selling of alcohol to minors; removes drinks containing alcohol from vending machines; bans liquor from all workplaces; forbids selling wine, beer, and hard liquor at sporting events from one hour before the event starts until it is over;

prohibits stores and gas stations from selling alcohol between 9 p.m. and 7 a.m.; outlaws the selling of hard liquor in bars before 10 a.m.; and requires that establishments selling alcoholic beverages have at least two soft drinks on their menus that cost the same as, or less than, the cheapest alcoholic drink.

Not everyone agrees that the bill is a good idea or that it will make a dent in the alcoholism problem. Zmago Jelincic, head of the Slovenian Nationalist Party, believes "it will be bad for Slovenian citizens, for the economy, and for the indigenous culture of which a glass or two will always be a part." In the cities, workers like to start their day at a café with coffee, a bun, and a glass or two of *sadjevec* (SAD-yea-vetz), a liquor made from mixed fruits. In rural areas there is a deep-rooted tradition of home brewing of wine, beer, and various liqueurs. Alcoholism is likely to remain a major Slovenian problem in spite of laws that are passed to curb it.

In 2001 a World Health Organization (WHO) report stated that among youths in Slovenia aged 15 to 16, twice as many boys as girls drunk to excess by age 13.

Many urban Slovenian families are small, with only one or two children per family. Rural families tend to have more children. Children and students are entitled to free health-care.

THE COMMON GOOD

Despite its problems, there are many benefits to living in Slovenia. Programs for people's welfare are not merely government policy, they are part of the value system embraced by the Slovenian people. In a popularly aggressive free-market economy, Slovenians treasure the unique programs of their social welfare state.

More than 25 percent of Slovenia's GDP is spent on social welfare. Roughly half of this goes to the pension and disability insurance system. The system provides social security for retired men over age 63, and retired women over age 61, with supplements for nonworking family members. It also covers people with disabilities who are unable to work and pays death benefits where indicated.

Health insurance is compulsory in Slovenia. It is paid for by the insured, their employers, and other contributors and is overseen by the Institute of Health Insurance of Slovenia. Mutual Health Insurance, which manages the plan for the 1.1 million Slovenians with health insurance policies, is a nonprofit organization owned by the insured. All plan members are guaranteed access to health services, medicines and prescription drugs, technical aid, nursing services where necessary, and other costs. The Institute of Health Insurance contributes over 7 percent of the GDP annually to keep the program going.

Slovenia's health-care program provides free examinations for children, students, and pregnant women. Women are eligible for counseling concerning family planning, contraception, pregnancy, and childbirth. Under Slovenia's Family Income Act, they also receive cash compensation during maternity leave. Mothers—and fathers if necessary— are granted leave with pay for purposes of child care.

Under Slovenia's Civil Procedure Act, there is a system of free legal assistance for people in need, including defendants and claimants in lawsuits as well as defendants in criminal cases. All legal costs, including lawyer's fees and procedural charges, are covered.

Such measures provide a needed sense of security for Slovenians. Throughout their history they have been ruled as a part of other nations—an empire, a patched together monarchy, a Communist state—with different ethnic identities. In the truest sense, they are now a new nation. At last, as President Janez Drnovsek told his people, "we have reached consensus on the basic values; we have created a safe, socially just and economically successful, tolerant country, which has its place on the economic scene and, most importantly, is forward-looking."

Retired Slovenian men over the age of 63 are entitled to social security.

LIFESTYLE

THE PEOPLE OF Slovenia have an easygoing confidence in their country and their way of life. This confidence combines with pride in the country's great natural beauty and a healthy economy. Slovenes welcome visitors from other countries, and many families open their homes to tourists and business travelers.

From the 14th century until 1918, Slovenia was almost constantly under the rule of the Austro-Hungarian Empire. This history had a lasting influence on the Slovenian way of life. The great flowering of Austrian culture, centered in Vienna in the 18th and 19th centuries, had a particularly strong impact on Slovenia's culture—its art, music, and theater—and even on foods and clothing styles. In western Slovenia, however, the proximity to Italy is evident in daily life. Some border towns, like Piran and Koper, are even bilingual, with signs and many documents in Italian as well as Slovenian, even though only about 3,000 people of Italian descent live in Slovenia.

LIFE IN LJUBLJANA

Half of Slovenia's people live in cities, and the capital—Ljubljana—is by far the largest with about 260,000 residents.

The pace of life in Ljubljana is slower and more relaxed than cities in the United States or western Europe. In addition, the city has a youthful aura, largely because nearly 50,000 students attend the University of Ljubljana. This youthful, modern lifestyle is seen in the more than twenty Internet cafes, where people can catch up on e-mail or research online.

Above: **Outdoor cafés are popular places for Slovenes to chat and have a drink together, especially when the weather is good.**

Opposite: **Many families bring their children to water parks, like this one in Brezice, on weekends.**

In Ljubljana, Slovenia's largest city, the majority of families live in apartments, some of which are converted mansions that date back centuries.

The university neighborhood is also identified by the large numbers of bicycles and motor scooters, as well as the percentage of people carrying laptops, cell phones, or CD players with headsets.

Ljubljana is a prosperous city, and most people have white-collar jobs in the many government offices, at the university, and with the many cultural institutions. Daily living patterns would seem quite familiar to most Americans. After a simple breakfast, kids rush off to school and adults take public transportation to work.

Evenings and weekends are a time for leisurely shopping in the many specialty shops or in the open-air produce market. Families and couples enjoy strolling through the narrow, winding streets of Old Town, where attractive old buildings are painted in soft pastel colors, and every turning presents a new picture-postcard scene. People also gravitate to Tivoli Park, where a popular recreation center offers swimming pools, tennis courts, bowling alleys, and a roller-skating rink.

Slovenes have a great fondness for concert music, opera, and dance. The major performance center, Cankarjev Don, has a schedule of nearly 700 events each year. Young people flock to a number of nightspots, featuring folk music, jazz, rock, and rap.

OTHER URBAN CENTERS

Slovenia's second largest city is Moribar, located only a few miles from the Austrian border. The strong Austrian influence is evident in family meals, which are likely to include Austrian specialties, like *klobasa* (klo-BA-sa), or sausage, and *zavitek* (za-VEE-tek), or strudel, along with more traditional Slovenian dishes, like the ever-present soup. This small city of less than 100,000 is more industrial that Ljubljana, so many men and women are employed in light industries. Moribar is also in the heart of Slovenia's wine-making region. Dozens of vineyards and wineries offer employment while also adding to the country's scenic beauty.

A few smaller cities are basically factory towns, like Jesenice, where about half the workers are employed in steel mills, and Kranj, a town of textile mills. Koper, a city of only 24,000 people, is Slovenia's major port. Life here is centered around the ports and tourist trade.

Internet cafés are not common in Ljubljana, but Internet terminals can sometimes be found at local bars and cafés, where young people socialize. About 10 percent of Ljubljana's population are university students who attend the University of Ljubljana.

RURAL LIFE

Slovenia's population is almost evenly divided between urban and rural. The rural way of life shows a good deal of variety, depending in large part on location. In western Slovenia, for example, the villages of the Julian Alps are very much like the mountain villages of Italy and Switzerland. Farm families raise sheep, goats, and dairy cattle, while other villagers work in the large resort hotels and ski schools. Almost everyone in this region is a skier or hiker, or both.

Many rural families live in other resort areas. The town of Bled, for example, located on a spectacular glacial lake, is a world-famous resort, and the life of people living here is geared to the tourist industry. Many open their homes to tourists and have been operating bed-and-breakfasts for several generations.

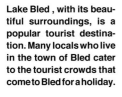

Lake Bled , with its beautiful surroundings, is a popular tourist destination. Many locals who live in the town of Bled cater to the tourist crowds that come to Bled for a holiday.

Slovenia is also well known for the healing properties of its springs. Spas have been attracting people from all over Europe since Roman times, and there are fifteen major spas in operation today. Young people who are interested in alternative medicine often seek work at the spas or start massage parlors or beauty salons.

More traditional rural life is found throughout Slovenia's farm region, most of it in fertile river valleys. Many of the farms are run as cooperatives, a legacy of Communist days, and this allows farm families to pool their resources for special needs like farm machinery.

In addition to wheat, corn, and other grains, farm families raise a variety of animals, including chickens, geese, sheep, goats, and dairy cattle. In addition, almost every farm has grapevines, both for the fruit and for wine making.

Many Slovenian farm families belong to the Association of Tourist Farms, a unique organization that invites tourists to spend several days living on a working farm in the countryside. Rural tourism is well-developed in Slovenia.

RITES OF PASSAGE

In the past, events in an individual's life were regulated by the Sacraments of the Roman Catholic Church. In modern Slovenia, the involvement of the Church is much less than it was before the Communist era. About 70 percent of the people are members of the Church, and these families adhere to most of the Holy Sacraments, especially baptism, First Communion, and marriage.

Parents are generally conscientious about having their children baptized, and they are strict in having children prepare for First Communion. First Communion is an important coming-of-age occasion, marking the child's entrance into the Roman Catholic Church.

As lifestyle become increasingly secular, church attendance becomes more casual. Even the Sacrament of marriage is not adhered to as closely as in the past, and each year more couples choose to be married to civil ceremonies, rather than in church service. Weddings are still an important occasion, however, with lavish parties usually held in a restaurant or hall.

EDUCATION

Slovenia boasts one of the highest literacy rates in the world, with virtually everyone over the age of ten able to read and write. Education is free and compulsory for all children between the ages seven and fourteen. More than half the student population now receives at least some education beyond high school.

Most Slovenes are fluent in at least one foreign language, and many people can speak and read two or three other languages. The most popular languages are English, especially among young people, German (the language of Austria); Magyar (Hungarian); Italian; and Croatian.

The University of Ljubljana, founded in 1595, is considered one of the best in Europe. There are more than thirty other institutions scattered throughout the country.

The University of Ljubljana, Slovenia's first university, was established in 1919.

RELIGION

THE SLOVENIAN constitution guarantees freedom of religious practice and expression in private and in public. No person can be compelled to admit his religious or nonreligious beliefs. There is no state religion. The main religion in Slovenia is Roman Catholicism. Other faiths are observed, and there is a significant portion of the population that does not follow any organized religion.

THE ROMAN CATHOLIC CHURCH

Historically, Catholicism has been a major influence on the culture of Slovenia. It is present in almost all Slovenian art, literature, poetry, architecture, and crafts. Catholicism has become embedded in the national

Left: **Three women head toward a small rural church in the countryside to attend Mass.**

Opposite: **The Church of the Assumption is located on a small island in the center of Lake Bled. The church was built in the 17th century.**

A Roman Catholic priest celebrates Mass. About 71 percent of Slovenia's population are Roman Catholic.

character and influences the everyday life of the people, even those who are non-Catholics or nonbelievers in any faith. However, although Slovenia is a Catholic country, only about 57 percent of the people say they are practicing Catholics. That is roughly 14 percent lower than those who said they were practicing Catholics in 1991, at the time that Slovenia was separating from Communist Yugoslavia.

Roman Catholics, like most other Christians, worship God, his son Jesus Christ, and the Holy Spirit. A belief in free will is key to Catholicism. Rituals of confession, repentance, and redemption play a large part in the Catholic faith. The priests and nuns who do the work of the church are required to take vows of celibacy. The head of the Roman Catholic Church is the pope, who is regarded as God's holy spokesman, and whose declarations are considered infallible.

In Slovenia, as in other nations that are considered to be Catholic countries, the Church stands firmly against contraception and abortion. Divorce is frowned upon. The Slovenian Catholic Church is a patriarchal structure. Some feminists in Slovenia's urban areas view Church doctrine as sexist. This may be one reason why the falloff in Catholic church attendance is greatest in the cities. Disillusionment with the Church is greatest among intellectuals and members of the upper classes. Older people, particularly in rural areas, are offended by attempts to reform Catholicism and resentful of non-Latin masses and modernized services. They are among those drawn to the more emotional approach of the Evangelical Protestant churches.

Despite a drop in membership, the Catholic Church still remains a power in Slovenian daily life. It exerts an influence in government, schools, and the common Slovenian morality. Those who have left the Church may not want to return to it, but neither do they want to do away with it.

The Roman Catholic Church is every bit as important to the Slovenian national identity and lifestyle as their Slovenian heritage.

Catholic churches in Slovenia are often decorated with beautiful statues and paintings of Jesus Christ and the saints. This fresco in a church in Bohinj depicts St. John the Baptist.

NONBELIEVERS AND UNAFFILIATED

When queried about their religious affiliation in 2002, over 300,000 (15.7 percent of Slovenians) refused to reply. While there may be other reasons, it is possible that many, if not most, of those who refused to state a religious preference are nonbelievers. Because of Slovenia's past role in Communist Yugoslavia, where "state atheism" was urged on the people and Socialist philosopher Karl Marx claimed that "religion is the opiate of the people," a Slovenian who today admits to not having a religious belief risks being labeled a Communist.

Nevertheless, in addition to those who refused to answer, nearly 200,000 Slovenians (10.1 percent of the population) defined themselves as atheists, while about 300 defined themselves as agnostics. This makes atheists one of the largest groups in Slovenia, second only to Roman Catholics. Atheists don't believe that there is any higher power, while agnostics believe it is simply impossible to know if there is or is not a God, or a future life. Some of these nonbelievers may be holdovers from the days of Communism, but others seem to be rebelling against what they perceive to be the inflexible belief systems of all organized religions.

ISLAM

Islam has one of the two fastest-growing congregations in Slovenia with over 47,000 followers (2.4 percent of the population). Muslims have been settling in Slovenia in increasing numbers over the past five decades, particularly since the outbreak of war in Bosnia and Kosovo. Both a new influx of Muslim refugees and a high birth rate have spurred an increase in the Muslim population of Slovenia.

The Islamic religion was founded by the prophet Muhammad in 610 c.e. Like Christianity and Judaism, it is a monotheistic religion, meaning that

Muslims believe in one God, whom they call Allah. Indeed, Islam acknowledges a common background with these religions, embracing such biblical figures as Adam, Noah, Moses, and Jesus. For Muslims, Muhammad is a prophet sent by God just as those prophets were. Just as Christians and Jews live by Holy Scripture, Muslims follow the Koran, which spells out the rules for ethical and moral conduct in life.

In Slovenia, Muslims, as either new immigrants or refugees, hold down the lowest paying jobs, often doing work that native Slovenes do not wish to do. They are not as yet very well organized. While they have prayer centers, they have not yet been granted government permission to erect any mosques in Slovenia.

Muslim girls attend a religious class.

A small shrine bearing a crucifix is located in front of an Eastern Orthodox church in Postojna.

THE EASTERN ORTHODOX CHURCH

The Eastern Orthodox Christians of Slovenia are almost as numerous as the Muslims, with a total of over 45,000 believers (2.3 percent of the population). They are both connected to the Roman Catholic Church and distinct from it. They follow different rites and Sacraments from those of Roman Catholicism and do not recognize the pope as their leader.

Although the rites of Eastern Orthodox Christians tend to be more elaborate than those of Roman Catholics, in other respects the Eastern religion is more relaxed. For instance, clergy are permitted to marry and have children. Divorce and remarriage are not condemned, but a remarriage ceremony must include prayer and repentance for the sin of divorce.

The Eastern Orthodox community in Slovenia includes a large number of Serbs who migrated there in search of work or in flight from Croat repression. Many of them are former officers and soldiers of what was the Yugoslav army. They have settled mostly in urban areas.

OTHER FAITHS

Less than 20,000 Slovenians (1.1 percent of the population) follow other religions than those discussed above. The largest of these groups are Evangelicals, with some 14,000 members (0.8 percent of the population). Each of the other religious groups—non-Evanglical Protestants, non-Protestant Christians, Buddhists, Hindus, various minor sects, and Jews (almost 60 years after the Holocaust, there are fewer than 100 Jews left in Slovenia)—account for 0.1 percent or less of the Slovenian population.

Nevertheless, in August 2003 the government of Slovenia took steps to register some of these groups as religious institutions. This granted them the same rights and exemptions as mainstream Slovenian religions. Among those recognized were the Tibetan Buddhist Dharmaling association and the city of Celje's Calvary Chapel Protestant Church. The Hindu community in Ljubljana anticipates recognition in the near future, and is already beginning to build a small temple.

MARIBOR SYNAGOGUE

Maribor Synagogue has recently been restored by the city of Maribor and the Slovenian Ministry of Culture, and is a monument of outstanding cultural value. The synagogue is one of the three oldest Jewish religious structures in Europe.

Between the period of the Holocaust and the present, the building had been used as a church. Now it will be open as a museum, with exhibits depicting Jewish life and history, and will be a center of Jewish cultural heritage.

HOLY SITES

The religious buildings of Slovenia provide visible evidence of the effect of faith on the tradition and culture of the people. Many of these structures are centuries old, and are maintained as national treasures. Others have been lovingly restored. Among the most hallowed are the following:

Ursuline Church of the Holy Trinity in the center of Ljubljana was built in 1726. It is famous for a beautiful multicolored altar made of African marble.

The Cathedral of St. Nazarius is on the city square in the seaport of Koper. Most of the structure dates from the 18th century, but some of it has been retained from buildings of earlier times. The Cathedral tower, known as City Tower, dates back to the 14th century. The top is reached by a long staircase, and the view is spectacular. The interior of the cathedral is richly decorated with marble columns and religious paintings. The cathedral also contains the sarcophagus, or tomb, of Saint Nazarius himself.

The Church of the Annunciation of Our Lady stands on Kostanjevica Hill, in Nova Gorica. The hill rises 469 feet (143 m) above the border with Italy, and there is a sweeping view of the countryside valleys from the church. Attached to the church is a 17th-century Franciscan monastery containing many treasures from olden times. The last members, the 19th-century French royal family, the Bourbons, are buried in a crypt beneath the church.

The Church of the Holy Trinity in the mining town of Idrija was built in 1500. Legend has it that the church was built atop a mercury mine discovered by a local tub maker. The mine, one of the largest of its kind in the world, was the reason that the city of Idrija grew up around it.

The Chapter Church of Novo Mesto is said to "rise above the town like a swan." The church dates back to 1493, and is famous for its altar image of Saint Nicholas, which many consider to be the most important monument in the history of Slovenian art. The church also contains a 16th century work by the noted Italian painter Tintoretto.

This is only a sampling of the rich religious architecture of Slovenia. The country is dotted with remarkable buildings, large and small, demonstrating the role that faith has played in Slovenia's history.

LANGUAGE

THE SLOVENIAN LANGUAGE is a South Slavic tongue written in the Roman alphabet. The words are closely related to Croatian and Serbian words, but not interchangeable with them. Slovenian grammar is extremely complicated and has many cases, genders, and tenses.

GERMANIZATION

Through much of the country's history, Slovenian was a secondary language kept alive by determined scholars like the author Primoz Trubar, the grammarian Anton Janezic, and others. During the 600 years Slovenia was ruled by the Austro-Hungarian Empire, the German language was imposed on the population, and Slovenian was looked down upon as a dialect spoken mostly by peasants. With the Nazi occupation of World War II, German, as well as Italian in some sections of the country, was insisted upon by the occupying forces.

There has been, to a significant extent, a Germanization of the Slovenian language. Many German words and phrases have made their way into conversational use. Most of them, over time, have been distorted into what Slovenes regard as their own words and phrases, but their origins are unmistakable. The German influence is particularly evident when it come to slang or colloquial speech.

Above: **Two university students stop to chat on a bridge in Ljubljana.**

Opposite: **A woman reads the local newspaper.**

Graffiti on a low wall in Ljubljana says "I love you Slovenia."

ALPHABET AND DIALECT

The Slovenian alphabet has 25 letters. Five of the letters are vowels and 20 are consonants. There is no *q, w, x,* and *y*. However, there are two versions of *c*, two versions of *s*, and two versions of *z*. The words that are formed often string consonants together in ways that seem unnatural to non-Slovenian eyes and ears.

According to an old saying, if you don 't have a dialect, you don 't have a language. There are at least 32 dialects in the Slovenian language. They vary from region to region with a *vzhodno* (wsh-OD-no) dialect spoken in eastern Slovenia, a *zahadno* (za-HOD-no) patois prevailing in the west, an *osrednje* (o-SRED-nee) slang used in the central region, and a *primorsko* (pree-MORE-sko) dialect favored in the areas near the Adriatic seacoast. Dialect speakers use the same Slovenian language but often arrange sentences and pronounce words in very different ways. It's similar to the difference between the speech of Appalachia and that of New York City, or between the French of rural Quebec and that of Paris.

PRIMOZ TRUBAR, AUTHOR

In a nation where 72 percent of the people are Roman Catholic and the 19,000 Protestants make up only 1 percent of the population, it is remarkable that Primoz Trubar should be hailed as the father of Slovenian literature. He was, after all, the founder and first superintendent of the Protestant Church of Slovenia. However, he was also the scholar who turned the Slovenian dialect into a structured language and the author of the first printed book in Slovenian.

Primoz Trubar was born in the village of Rasica in Slovenia on June 9, 1508. His parents were religious Roman Catholics, and a deep commitment to God was instilled in him as a child. He attended school in Rijeka from 1522 to 1524, and then went to Salzburg, Germany, to continue his education. From Salzburg, he went to Trieste to further his religious experience. He came under the influence of Bishop Pietro Bonomo, a member of the emerging humanist movement. The young Trubar mingled with humanist writers, and was swayed by their views. In particular, he became a disciple of Erasmus, who is considered by many historians to be one of the greatest philosophical thinkers of the Middle Ages.

Having enrolled at the University of Vienna in 1528 to further both his religious and philosophical studies, Primoz Trubar left after two years. His time there, however, had deepened his religious commitment, and so he returned to Slovenia and became a preacher. His love of God was deep; but under the humanist influence, he began leaning away from the Roman Catholic faith and toward Protestantism.

In 1547, labeled a heretic, Primoz Trubar was expelled from Slovenia. He went to Rothenberg, Germany, to preach the gospel as a Protestant minister. While there, he wrote *Catechismus* (in 1550) and *Abecedarium* (in 1555), the first books ever written in the Slovenian language. *Catechismus* was published in 1550 in Tubingen, Germany. He produced 25 more books in Slovenian during the years that followed. The most important is a Slovenian translation of the New Testament.

Trubar died in Derendingen, Germany, on June 28, 1586. He was 78 years old. Today the Protestant exile Primoz Tubar's image appears on Slovenian currency (*right*), and more than 400 years after his death, he remains the nation's most honored author.

SECOND LANGUAGES

The manner of speaking can be as important as the words in Slovenian conversation. A certain formality prevails when city people address one another; in rural areas speech is apt to be guarded, and body language takes on added importance. In both city and countryside, politeness and good manners prevail.

Most Slovenes speak a second language. The most common one is German. Italian, Croatian, and Serbian are also understood and spoken in different parts of the country. In the major cities, English is fast becoming the second language of choice. This is particularly true among young people, as American films, music, and clothing are being assimilated into the culture. American slang, in particular, may be heard in the streets of Ljubljana, and other major cities.

THE FREISING MANUSCRIPTS

Brizinski spomeniki is the Slovenian name for the Freising Manuscripts (*below*), the oldest written text in the Slovenian language. They consist of three sermons on sin and repentance and are believed to have been written by the Slovenian bishop Abraham between 957 and 994 A.D. Four parchment leaves and a quarter of a page have been preserved.

Bishop Abraham owned, and at times lived on, a large estate in Central Slovenia. He also served the Roman Catholic Church in Freising, Germany, where he is believed to have written the manuscripts. The bishop died over 1,000 years ago on May 26, 994.

In 1807 papers from the Freising Diocese were transferred to the Munich National Library to be examined. It was during the examination that the Freising Manuscripts were discovered.

The Slovene Academy of Sciences and Arts published a facsimile of the Freising Manuscripts in 1992 and made it available for public viewing. In 1994 the Bank of Slovenia issued three limited edition coins—one gold, one silver, and one made of a copper-zinc alloy—to commemorate the Freising Manuscripts. Imprinted on these coins, using the original Latin script, are the words *Glagolite ponaz*—the Slovenian words with which the first Freising Manuscript begins. Roughly translated, it means "Speak Our Language."

ARTS

GREATLY INFLUENCING the Slovenian culture and lifestyle, the arts—painting, sculpture, literature, drama, music, dance, and film—play a major role in the emerging consciousness of this relatively new nation.

LITERATURE

Poetry prevails in the literary tradition of Slovenia. France Preseren (1800-1849), thought by some to be the leading European representative of romanticism, established the tradition for the Slovenian poets who followed him. Long after Preseren's death, Tomaz Salamun's poem *Eclipse* was still bitterly lamenting the absence of Slovenian nationhood and proclaiming that "I grew tired of the image of my tribe and moved out." Preseren's romantic despair lives on in the poetic reflection on doomed love by Uros Zupan, which asks, "And what is left? A quiet room, the smell of the carpet which will fill the room long after we have each gone our own way . . ." The new young poets of Slovenia carry on this tradition with works that reflect both the bittersweet romantic and idealistically nationalist influences of Preseren's verses.

Today's Slovenian novelists tend to be more political and less lyric than the poets. They take their lead from Ivan Cankar (1876–1918), who used deceptively simple language and a frequently satiric style to criticize Slovenian society and politics. However, the styles of those who followed him have varied. In modern times Katarina Marincic's novel *Prikrita Harmonija* (*A Concealed Harmony*), a family novel set in World War I, has

Above: **Many works by Slovenian writers and poets can be found at Slovenia's National and University Library in Ljubljana. The library was designed by Joze Plecnik.**

Opposite: **An artist's workshop.**

THE GREATEST SLOVENIAN POET

The life, legend, and poetry of France Preseren are in many ways a reflection of the Slovenian national character. His romanticism, pessimism, and lyrical flights of fancy echo both the history, myths, and artistic patterns of the nation. He is considered the father of modern Slovenian literature.

France Preseren was born on December 3, 1800, in Vrba, Slovenia. At that time, Slovenia was part of the Austro-Hungarian Empire and was benefitting from educational reforms instituted by the Empress Maria Theresa. These reforms had increased literacy and created a reading public hungry for works in their native language. France Presersen was destined to satisfy that hunger.

As a boy, France went to live with an uncle in Kopanje. He went to elementary school there and returned home only during holidays. He later continued his studies in Ljubljana, and when he was 21 years old, he went to Vienna, where he studied law.

In Vienna, France came into contact with what was known as the romantic movement in European literature. He was much influenced by it, and when he returned to Slovenia as a civil servant and lawyer in Ljubljana and Kranj, he began writing poetry. Life during this period was a struggle for him; his work was tedious, and the pay, only barely enough to sustain him.

During the 1830s Preseren fell hopelessly in love and suffered painful rejection. In 1835 his closest friend Majija Cop died a sudden death. France became deeply depressed and came close to committing suicide. He was described during this time as gentle, good-hearted, romantic, and freethinking. He was physically attractive with wavy black hair and deep gray eyes, an image that fit well with the soulful feelings some of his poetry evoked.

His unhappy love affair inspired *Sonetni Venec* (*Garland of Sonnets*), which reflects not just his personal misery but the national consciousness of a subjugated people. The epic poem *Krst pri Savici* (*The Baptism by the Savica*), which was dedicated to the memory of Majija Cop illustrates a peculiarly Slovenian combination of such traits as patriotism, pessimism, and resignation. *Zdravljica* (*A Toast*), by Preseren, encompasses both the yearning for independence of Slovenes before they attained it and the nation's commitment to peace. The seventh stanza, set to the music of Stanko Premrl, was adopted by the Slovenian Assembly as the national anthem of the country. It reflects a pacifist sentiment unusual in the nationalistic anthems of many other countries. France Presersen died on February 8, 1849, not yet 50 years old. The themes and structure of his work set the standards for the Slovenian poets who followed. His poems are taught in the schools, and he is recognized throughout the land as "the greatest Slovenian poet."

been compared to the work of Proust. Andrej Blatnik's short stories have been likened by reviewers to those of Raymond Carver. Reflecting on the work of up-and-coming Slovenian authors, Blatnik predicts that "Slovenian literature will be more closely connected with the fate of world literature in the future than it has been to date." This is perhaps borne out by the success of Drago Jancar's novel *Mocking Desire*.

The famous Slovenian playwright Drago Jancar. His novel *Mocking Desire* stands out as the most frequently translated work of Slovenian fiction.

THEATER

Drago Jancar, born in Maribor in 1948, is also one of Slovenia's leading playwrights. His drama *Halstatt*, a dark comedy dealing with questions of truth and illusion, contains elements reminiscent of the works of both Samuel Beckett and Tennessee Williams. *Halstatt* was recently performed in Great Britain. Along with Jancar's other plays, it enjoys frequent revivals in Slovenia.

The first plays in the Slovenian language were written by Anton Tomaz Linhart in the 18th century. In modern times, along with Jancar the best-known Slovenian playwrights are Emil Filipcic, Evald Flisar, and Dane

Theater is a part of the Slovenian arts scene. Many theater events are held annually.

Jazc. *Grmace* (*Rocky Peak*), by Jazc, is the story of a patricide foiled by the intended victim's natural death, and has been called "vigorously Brechtian" by critics. The well-known Slovenian actor Jernej Sugman has played the lead in *Grmace*. Emil Filipcic's comedies are popular with theatergoers in Slovenia, while Evald Flisar's psychological dramas elicit both praise and controversy.

Theater is part of Slovenia's national culture program. The nation's first professional theater was founded in the 18th century in Ljubljana, when Slovenia was still part of the Austro-Hungarian Empire. Today there is a Slovenian National Theater in both Ljubljana and Maribor. There are other theaters, including puppet theaters for children, in cities and towns throughout Slovenia. On average, about 100 professional productions take place each year.

The film director talks to some of the actors during the shooting of the Slovenian film *Oda Preseren.*

FILM

Only recently have Slovenian films attracted attention from the rest of the moviegoing world. The breakthrough came in March 2000, when *Vleru* (*Idle Running*), directed by Janez Burger, aroused interest at the New Directors/New Films Festival at Lincoln Center in New York City. There followed a retrospective of six Slovenian productions at the BAMcinamatek in Brooklyn, New York. These films dealt with a wide range of subjects, including the war in Bosnia, relationships, alcoholism, drug use, dysfunctional families, abortion, the buying and selling of human beings, and the uniquely Slovenian national character. One recent Slovenian film, *Oda Preseren* (*Ode to the Poet*), delves into the myths and realities of the Slovenian cultural hero France Preseren.

PAINTING

During the Renaissance and the overlapping baroque period, from roughly the 13th through the 17th century, Slovenian painters and sculptors were influenced by art movements originating in Italy and, to a lesser extent, the Austro-Hungarian Empire.

Beautiful oils with mostly mythic and religious themes rendered by Slovenian painters can be viewed in many of the nation's churches, castles, and galleries. Included are works by baroque painters Giulio Quaglio, Franc Jelovsek, Johann Caspar Waginger, and Anton Lerchinger. Several works by the best-known Slovenian painter of the period, Valentin

Painted beehive panels, an example of Slovenian art in the countryside. These panels were painted in the 1970s and are located in a park near the city of Kranj.

Janez Metzinger, are hung in the Chapter Church of St. Nicholas in Dolenjska.

The life of baroque painter Anton Cebej is shrouded in mystery. Neither his date of birth nor the date of his death are known. It is believed that he came from Sturje, in the Vipava region of Slovenia, and that he painted between 1750 and 1774. He was influenced by the baroque Venetian painters, but his work has a central European intensity. Three of his paintings—*Corpus Christi-Sanguis Christi, St. Leopold*, and *St. Florian*—hang in the National Gallery in Ljubljana. They are characterized by subtle colors and powerful spirituality.

During the romantic movement in art (late 18th to mid-19th century) the landscape art of Anton Karinger flourished in Slovenia. He was followed by Ivana Kobilica, Slovenia's best-known female painter, who produced most of her 200 oil paintings during the decade of the 1880s. Her work, which hangs in art galleries throughout Europe, illustrates the crossover from the realism that replaced romanticism to the impressionist school, which would begin to flower around the turn of the century. During that period Ivan Grohar also made the transition from realism to impressionism with paintings of Slovenian landscapes and peasant life.

Impressionism evolved into a more abstract expressionism in Slovenia following World War I. From the 1920s through the 1950s Franz Kralj and Verno Pilon were the leading Slovenian expressionist artists. Kralj's paintings, along with his woodcuts and sculptures, may be viewed at the Museum of Modern Art in Ljubljana. Much of Pilon's more surrealist work, including both paintings and photographic studies, is in the Pilon Galerie in the Slovenian town of Ajdovscina, where he was born.

This fresco of a scene from the life of St. John the Baptist is an example of the religious art that can be found in many of Slovenia's old churches.

SCULPTURE

Modern Slovenian sculpture has progressed along much the same path as painting. Typical is the work of Tobias Putrih, a young Slovene whose work created some controversy when it was recently exhibited at the Max Protech Gallery in New York.

Defined as a "conceptualist," Putrih uses familiar objects in his sculptures. One called *Unity* is cobbled together out of cardboard egg crates decorated with actual eggs. Others are constructions of sticks forming modular networks that define nothing but space.

Another, praised by critics, is entitled *Roxy vs. Capital*, and consists of a laminated cardboard construction of what looks like moonscape cliffs. These are meant to represent the screens of two famous movie theaters. Like that of other modern Slovenian sculptors, Putrih's work must be seen and seriously considered before rendering a final judgment.

This modern school of sculpture is a far cry from the Slovenian sculpture of the past. Many, if not most, of the sculptures from early periods that are to be seen in Slovenia's churches, castles, homes, and

THE IRWIN GROUP

In 1954 painters in Ljubljana founded the IRWIN group, which eventually evolved into the New Slovenian Art Movement. The works of many IRWIN group painters gained worldwide attention. Among those responsible for spreading the influence of Slovenian art to other countries are Roman Uranjek, Dusan Mandie, Miran Mohar, and Andrej Savski. Examples of their works hang in Venice, Rotterdam, New York, and some other U.S. cities. They also may be viewed in museums, galleries, and art centers throughout Slovenia. Abstract to the eye, IRWIN art is based on a retro principle that incorporates a variety of painting styles along with historical imagery and avant-garde techniques. In the 21st century Slovenian painting has evolved into an individualistic use of forms and colors that challenges the eye and invites interpretation by the viewer.

public squares were created by unknown craftspersons. Superlative examples of these early periods make up the collection of 850 pieces on view at the National Gallery in Ljubljana. These include urns and busts from the Romanesque period, elaborately decorated Gothic pieces in both stone and bronze, and unusual baroque wood sculptures. Also on view are the monumental baroque sculptures of Veit Koniger and the late 19th century works of Ivan Zajc.

In more recent times the work of Stojan Bati has drawn international attention. He fought with the resistance during World War II, and kept an enemy's knife, which he subsequently used in producing his sculptures. More impressionist than abstract experiment, his work may be viewed in various Slovenian museums and art centers. Another famous Slovenian sculptor is Marjetica Potrc, who is also an architect. Her work was recently shown at the prestigious Guggenheim Museum in New York City.

MUSIC

Slovenian music dates back to the 16th century. That was when Jacobus Gallus Carniolus (1550-1591), also known as Jacobus Gallus and Jakob Petelin, wrote his first sacred compositions. A monk from Ribnica, Slovenia, Jacobus Gallus Carniolus's most notable work is the six-part *Opus musicum* designed as a musical series to go along with the annual worship program. Written for eight voices, the *Opus Musicum* contrasts with some of the other music that he wrote, including both rhythmic, madrigal-style melodies and a still much-performed funeral anthem titled *The Ways of Zion Do Mourn*.

By 1701 the Slovenian public's taste had shifted from church music to embrace the baroque compositions of the period, and the Slovenian Philharmonic Society was founded. Over the succeeding years, its

A Slovenian folk band performs during a festival at Lake Bohinj.

honorary members would include composers Ludwig van Beethoven, Niccolo Paganini, and Johannes Brahms. Subsequently, Gustav Mahler was musical conductor of the Ljubljana Provincial Theater for an entire year.

Perhaps Slovenia's best-loved composer is Hugo Wolf (1860-1903). He wrote 51 songs for the *Goethe Songbook*, which, together with 44 Spanish songs, are a major part of the Slovenian folk song heritage. He also wrote an opera, *Der Corregidor*, which was unsuccessful, as were several of his symphonic pieces. It was only when he began to use folktales and literature as an inspiration that his music truly flowered.

Slovenian music today is varied. The Ljubljana String Quartet regularly performs classical pieces on concert stages throughout Slovenia and abroad. The musical group Terrafolk includes classical, pop, and rock in its repertoire and jazzes up Romany, Irish, Klezmer, Mexican, and Slovenian music. Winners of the World Music 2003 Audience Award, the group's album *Jumper of Love* is a big hit in Europe. Another popular Slovenian vocal group is Katice. In collaboration with Slovenian pop singer Roberto Magnifico, they have come out with an album of 16 songs originating from different areas of Slovenia.

Slovenia's Philharmonic building is located in the heart of Ljubljana. It is home to the Slovene Philharmonic Orchestra.

THE NEANDERTHAL FLUTE Slovenian archeologist Ivan Turk made an astonishing discovery in 1995. Among the bone fragment remains of Europe's earliest prehuman cavemen—Neanderthals—he found a 5-inch (12-centimeter) length of carved bone from the thigh of a cave bear. The bone had been hollowed out, and had four well-rounded holes drilled into it. The holes were spaced apart precisely to form musical notes when breath was blown through one end of the bone. The notes were different when the holes were covered and uncovered in a variety of arrangements. It was soon determined that what Ivan Turk had found was a flute.

The bone of the cave bear was sent to New York City for analysis. The examination indicated that the teeth and the bone were between 43,000 and 82,000 years old, dating back to the Neanderthal Age. If that is true, then the Neanderthals were making music, and the very first music in the world was played on the Neanderthal Flute in the mountains of Slovenia. That would make Slovenia the oldest musical culture in the world.

DANCE

Folk dancing is festive in Slovenia, and colorful peasant costumes are often worn, particularly in the smaller towns. The dances themselves, while heavily influenced by the long Austro-Hungarian rule, also incorporate movements from Ukraine, Russia, Italy, and Serbia. The result is a melding of forms combining traditional movements with innovative techniques that can only be described as uniquely Slovenian.

There is also a tradition of ballet in Slovenia, which dates back to the 18th century cultural programs of the Austrian empress Maria Theresa. Today ballet is part of the national culture. Among the more prominent ballet companies are Fico Ballet and the Slovenian National Ballet.

THE MASTER BUILDER

Ljubljana, the capital of Slovenia, was virtually remade by the vision of architect Joze Plecnik. The parks and squares, the library, museum, and government buildings, the stadium, the bridges, and even the banks of the Ljubljanica River are all the result of Plecnik's 15-year project to redesign the city. Viewed as a whole, the Ljubljana of Plecnik is a testament to his theory that architecture must express the history of its setting through careful research. He advocated building to a human scale, by which he meant that the eventual user of the architecture must be taken into consideration along with history and setting when planning a structure.

Joze Plecnik was born on January 23, 1872, in Ljubljana. In the 1890s he went to Vienna, Austria, where he met Otto Wagner, author of the highly influential book *Modern Architecture*. Plecnik enrolled in the architecture department of the Academy of Fine Arts and studied under Wagner for three years. In 1921 Plecnik returned to Ljubljana as head of the architecture department at the new Ljubljana University. World War I had freed Slovenia from Austro-Hungarian rule, and there was a movement to express a national identity and culture through art, literature, and architecture. Plecnik was not only charged with educating the first generation of Slovenian architects but also with redesigning the nation's capital. He worked until World War II broke out. During that period his architecture established a Slovenian identity for the city. Plecnik resumed his work after the war.

In 1956 he died at age 84. His memorial is Ljubljana itself, a city of architectural images that epitomize the culture of Slovenia. One of his most memorable works is the Three Bridges (*below*).

LEISURE

SLOVENES ARE A high-energy people, and their leisure-time activities reflect this. They take to the outdoors for their recreation in both summer and winter. Whether skiing, hiking, and mountain climbing or swimming, rafting, and kayaking, it is the fresh air and the seasonal changes that define their relaxation. Slovenes live close to nature and relax in harmony with it.

WINTER SPORTS

Skiing is by far the most popular sport in Slovenia. One out of every four Slovenes is an active skier. All Slovenes take pride in the sport. Their proudest moment came on

Above: **A sports center allows Slovenes to enjoy sports indoors during winter. Slovenes also enjoy skiing or ice skating at this time of year.**

Opposite: **A group of young hikers enjoy the view from the summit of Visevnik, a mountain located in Gorenjska.**

October 7, 2000. That was the day that Davo Karnicar skied nonstop down Mount Everest, the world's highest mountain. He was the first person to ever descend from the 29,035 foot (8,856 m) crest of the mountain on skis.

From December to March the well-equipped ski resorts in the Julian Alps are booked to capacity. The most popular area is the Kranjska Gora winter sports center in the northwest corner of Slovenia, bordering Austria and Italy. Overlooking Triglav National Park, Kranjska Gora is famous for the World Ski Championship events and ski-jumping contests held there. Its Pianica ski jump is the world's first such site over 656 feet (200 m) high.

Vacationing Slovenes also go downhill sleigh riding at night on the torch-lit slopes of Kranjska Gora. During days when the ski runs can get overcrowded, the more adventurous climb the area's frozen waterfalls, using ice picks to grasp the ice. Those seeking less strenuous pleasures go ice-skating on nearby Lake Bled, surrounded by dense pine forests and towered over by the snowcapped Julian Alps.

SUMMERTIME ACTIVITIES

Slovenia's 29-mile (47-km) shoreline on the Adriatric Sea offers some of the best ocean swimming and snorkeling in Europe. Three of the beaches received the European Union Blue Flag in recognition of their ecological soundness and upkeep.

Not just Slovenes but vacationers from all over Europe flock to the clean and inexpensive hotels along these beaches in the warm weather. There are also private apartments available that provide changes of linen and cleaning services. These are very popular with Slovenian students, who pool their money and sometimes arrange seasonal shares with staggered visits for as many as a dozen or more occupants.

The beaches at Piran are a popular destination for locals and tourists.

There are many warm-weather activities available for older children vacationing in Slovenia. Summer camps, often located alongside one or another of the country's many lakes, offer a wide variety of programs. Some feature conventional athletics, water sports, crafts, and nature studies, while others specialize in specific disciplines. There are karate camps, soccer camps, computer camps, and camps devoted to gymnastics.

Both older children and young adults enroll in the ever-popular biking tours routed over various regions of the country. They cover areas from the the Julian Alps to the Skocjan Caves, from the Adriatic Sea to the capital city of Ljubljana, from the valleys of Slovenj Gradec to the artificial lakes of Podravje. Some of these bike tours are combined with nature studies. One of them is devoted to the capture and identification of the many different and beautiful species of butterflies in Slovenia.

Many Slovenes enjoy swimming in the country's lakes and rivers to cool off in the summer heat.

HIKERS AND BOATERS

Cycling and other strenuous outdoor activities are not limited to summertime. Spring and fall are also active periods for the many Slovenes who prefer to take their vacations before or after the summer influx of tourists. Hiking the alpine trails, or the forests of Koroska is pleasant in milder weather. Swimming alongside schools of trout in the crystal clear waters of the Lake Bohinj is only possible when the vacation crowds have thinned out.

Autumn and spring are also the seasons favored by boaters in Slovenia for exploring the coves and inlets of Slovenia's many lakes in kayaks and canoes. Braver kayakers will follow the white-water rafters into the rushing streams of the Soca, Mislinja, Kolpa, or Sava rivers. Some rafters will explore the underground rivers in the caves of southwest Slovenia. These sites also attract many spelunkers (cave explorers). Because of the

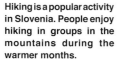

Hiking is a popular activity in Slovenia. People enjoy hiking in groups in the mountains during the warmer months.

unusual nature of the Slovenian cave complexes and the many fascinating specimens of both flora and fauna to be found there, spelunking has become an increasingly popular leisure activity for Slovenes.

SPECTATORS AND CLIMBERS

Both competitive sports and man-against-nature activities attract Slovenes of all ages. Many young people, both male and female join soccer teams that compete against each other in loosely organized leagues. Reportedly, 40 percent of the population is actively engaged in one sport or another.

Soccer, called football in Slovenia, is a spectator sport that draws large crowds. Fans are loyal and vocal, and support their teams strongly. In 2002 the Slovenian National Football Team qualified for the 2002 Football World Cup competition. Some Slovenian fans sold their cars and other valuable objects in order to fly to Japan to support the team. They were devastated when Brazil won the World Cup and Slovenia made an unexceptional showing.

Mountain climbing and rock climbing in the alpine regions of Slovenia can be dangerous pastimes. Many Slovenes in the hilly parts of the country are natural climbers. Others take to it as a challenge. The ultimate challenge for Slovenian climber Tomaz Homar back in November 1999 was Dhaulagiri mountain in north central Nepal. His solitary climb up the 15,000-foot (4,600-m) south face of Dhaulagiri was—in the words of a rival climber—crossing "the boundary of the impossible" into a "death zone." Homar's success made him a national hero and inspired a generation of Slovenes to take up mountain climbing.

Slovenian soccer player Zeljko Milinovic (*center*) vies for the ball from Paraguay's Roberto Acuna (*left*) as team player Amir Karic (*right*) looks on during a match between Slovenia and Paraguay at the Jeju World Cup Stadium in Korea at the 2002 FIFA World Cup.

GAMES

While Slovenian women participate in all of the sports and activities mentioned, the field in which they traditionally excel is gymnastics. From the time they are very small, Slovenian children are encouraged to train their bodies in calisthenics. In gymnastics suppleness is as important as strength, and Slovenian girls develop stretch exercise techniques at an early age. Gymnastics becomes part of their leisure-time routine, and once grown, most Slovenian women work out regularly. In the warm weather you can see small groups of women practicing their gymnastic skills in the parks and on the beaches of Slovenia.

A young gymnast stretches before class. Gymnastics is a popular sport for Slovenian girls, and many start learning gymnastics at a very young age.

Women are also increasingly taking up chess. Traditionally a game for men, it has always been taken seriously in Slovenia. Chess matches and tournaments are frequent. Chess players hunched over boards in outdoor cafes are a common sight in Slovenian cities. The two Polgar sisters, chess champions of Hungary, have inspired the women of Slovenia who are learning openings and gambits, coming up with moves to challenge the male dominance of the game.

Chess is not the only nonathletic leisure-time pursuit in Slovenia. In rural areas men and women play Preference, a pinochle-type game played with a deck of 32 cards. In the cities they are more likely to play Tarok. The Tarok deck has 54 cards, which break down into 22 trumps and four suits of eight cards. Children, using whatever deck is around, play nameless games similar to Go-Fish, or War.

Playing backgammon is another leisure activity at local bars.

FESTIVALS

SUMMER IS THE festival season in Slovenia, marked by many traditional and colorful celebrations. However, the symbol of Slovenian festivals is actually a springtime figure born of pagan legend who allegedly worked his supernatural powers to chase winter away. His name is Kurent, and today he is both a national symbol and a mythic presence at all Slovenian festivals.

THE BELLS OF KURENT

The legend of Kurent originated in Slovenia's oldest city of Ptuj. Now it is celebrated in many other cities and towns throughout Slovenia. The revels take place on Shrove Tuesday, 40 days before the start of Lent. On that day

Left: **Two girls dress up as clowns during the annual Ptuj carnival.**

Opposite: **A man dressed in a costume celebrates the Kurentovanje festival in Ptuj.**

111

A group of Slovenian girls dress up as Romany, or gypsies, for the carnival procession during the Kurentovanje festival, which pays homage to the Kurent, a mythical creature that is believed to chase away winter and welcome spring.

children and adults wearing traditional Kurent masks run through the streets skipping and jumping so that the bells they have hanging from their belts ring loudly enough to scare the cold winter away. Custom finds young girls in colorful peasant dresses offering handkerchiefs to those masquerading as Kurents. Housewives break clay pots at their feet for good luck and offer an age-old incantation: "Who tells a tale always adds a word." With this truth they acknowledge that the legend of Kurent grows from added word to added word, like Pinocchio's nose.

While Shrove Tuesday is the high point of the homage to Kurent, festivities take place during the days both before and after it. Revelers parade through the streets wearing a variety of masks called *laufarji*. These are modeled after creatures out of Slovenian mythology as well as caricatures of modern politicians. The main parades feature colorful floats and marching bands or strolling fiddlers. Carnivals vary from place to place. One of the most colorful is in Cerknika, where local tradition calls for a variety of witches' costumes.

Food plays a large part in the Kurent festivals. The start of the festivities used to be marked by cooking a pig's head; but with the years a certain squeamishness has developed, and today the kickoff meal is more likely to be smoked ham. The Friday before Shrove Tuesday is a day of fasting, but on Saturday savory cooking aromas once again fill the air. Fried doughnuts are traditional, and children go from door-to-door soliciting doughnuts, other goodies, or small sums of money. A very old ritual consists of giving wood logs to unmarried people, who then must donate money toward a sort of singles party. On Ash Wednesday, the day after Shrove Tuesday, a stuffed figure of Kurent is buried in a ceremony to mark the end of winter. Finally, the feasting concludes with the serving of the *potica* (po-TEE-tza), the traditional Slovenian dessert cake.

Slovenes dress up in the Kurent costume and take to the streets to dance. Kurent costumes can be made of straw or sheepskin, with cow bells attached to the waist.

MUSIC FESTIVALS

Music fills the valleys and bounces off the mountainsides of Slovenia during the months of July and August. Festivals of every musical genre compete with one another all summer long. Every city and village has a program to offer, and impromptu street performances are common.

The most famous cultural celebration is the International Summer Festival featuring not only music but theater and dance performances as well. These are held in both Ljubljana and Bled between the end of June and the beginning of September. During the same period Brezice, in the hills of the Posavje region, offers its annual Early Music Festival. This

Traditional bands provide music for folk festivals such as the Kraji Bal festival held at Lake Bohinj each year.

A group of Slovenian musicians practice for their performance in the courtyard of Borl Castle.

world-renowned event features music ranging from the medieval to Beethoven, performed on the authentic instruments of the relevant periods. From its beginning in 1983, under the artistic direction of Klemen Ramovs, it has attracted top international performers. Many of the Brezice concerts take place in the acoustically outstanding Knight's Hall, the high-ceilinged chamber of a Renaissance castle. Other performances are held in the Mokrice Castle, with its impressively decorated floors, and in the huge arcaded courtyard of the Kostanjevica monastery.

The Kostanjevica monastery is also known for its yearly summer cycle of concerts called Music from the Gardens of St. Frances. The concert is named for the work of Slovenian linguist and religious philosopher Stanislav Skrabec, who lived and worked in the monastery for 42 years. The cycle features a number of Slovenian musicians from Gorisko and Primorska, as well as musicians from Italy. Selections vary from baroque to the works of the romantic composers.

TRNFEST

A more varied, and more modern, event is the *Trnfest* (TERN-fest) series held every August in Trnovo. The lively five-week program, which is free, is usually packed with enthusiastic beer drinkers, making it a shoulder-to-shoulder experience of Slovenian socializing. The crowd is usually good-natured, and incidents of violence are rare.

A recent five-week trnfest series offered the following: *Fanfare Ciocarlia*, a 12-member Romany (gypsy) brass band playing traditional Romany rhythms combined with music from Macedonia and Bulgaria; *Teater Pozitiv*, a dance theater group based locally in Dijaski; *Zakarya*, offering jazz from France; and *Uzgin Uve*, a Hungarian presentation of Middle East folk music with cosmic sounds that include Tuvan throat singing and homemade wind instruments.

In addition to the concerts, trnfest offers weekly workshops in African dance, acting techniques, batik painting on clothing, and other disciplines. There are also Thursday afternoon creative workshops for children. Some evenings there are parties with professional or amateur deejays. In addition, there is a two-day weekend music festival, Street Explosion, devoted to urban street culture.

JAZZ, PUPPETS, AND COWS

One of the more unusual summer festivals is The Days of the Saxophone held in Nova Gorica. Saxophone players from all over the world flock to the Nova Gorica Cultural Center to hit the high notes during this unique jam session. The music tends to be mostly blues and traditional jazz.

Not just music but folklore, crafts, and local culture highlight the late June-early July Lent Festival in Slovenia's second largest city, Maribor. Summertime is also when the Maribor Puppet Theater hosts the International Puppet Festival, which attracts puppeteers from all over the world. Each year children of all ages and all language groups are entertained by new puppet plays.

In mid-September the mooing of the cows descending to the valleys from their high pasturelands heralds the *Kravij Bal* (Cows' Ball) festival in the Bohinj Valley. Platters of steaming food draw crowds. Once people have eaten and drunk their fill, the country-style folk dancing begins. As couples slip in and out of the various reels, the dancing continues nonstop until the weekend-long Cows' Ball is over.

Above: **Herdsmen lead their cows In a street procession during the Kravij Bal, or Cows' Ball, festival, which marks the return of the cows from high pasture. Slovenes wear traditional clothes during this festival.**

Opposite: **Two musicians perform on stage. The Trnfest features a variety of music, from folk to Middle Eastern tunes.**

CHESS, MOVIES, AND DRESSAGE

Slovenia hosts a variety of fall and winter festivals. In October, City of Women, an international festival of contemporary female artists, presents the works of women painters, sculptors, performance artists, plus a variety of other artistic endeavors produced by women. In October and November the Chess Olympics are held in Bled. Masters and often grand masters come from all over the world to compete against each other, and against Slovenian chess players, who have often trained from early childhood and who take their chess very seriously.

The Ljubljana International Film Festival is held in November. The aim of the festival is to introduce Slovenian audiences and visiting film buffs to the best movies—regardless of where they were produced, what the size of the budget was, or the stardom status of the cast. During the selection process special attention is paid to the work of new and as yet unrecognized directors. Following this festival, during the week of December 2-9, Slovenia's Festival of Gay and Lesbian Film (FGLF) is presented. In its 17th year, the FGLF was organized by one of Slovenia's leading poets, Brane Mozetic, along with a coalition of other leading gay activists concerned with creating an audience for films dealing with gay life.

Winter sports events begin in January with the World Cup Women's Slalom Races on the slopes of Maribor. These are followed by the International Dog Sled Race, which kicks off from Kranjska Gora at the foot of the Julian Alps in northwestern Slovenia and proceeds through the most beautiful of alpine valleys, the Zgornjesavska, a snow-covered area of legends and fairy tales. In March the Pianica slopes are the site of the World Championship Sky Flying and Ski Jumping Events, while Bled hosts the World Military Winter Games. The following month Bled is the site of the International Festival of Folk Dialect Choirs, while Ljubljana draws tourists to the VINO International Wine Fair. In June, Ljubljana's International Jazz Festival attracts jazz fans from all over Europe. Then, from June through September, in Lipica near the Italian border the World Cup International Dressage Competition is held.

Dressage is an exhibition of horsemanship in which the horse is put through a series of difficult movements by the very slight movements of its rider. It is an art form as precise as a ballet, and requires months of training for both horse and rider. The most famous horses of dressage competition are the all-white Lipizzaners, once the steeds of Austrian royalty and of the Emperor's Royal Guard. For hundreds of years horses bred in Lipica have been considered the créme de la créme of the Lipizzaner strain. The World Cup International Dressage Competition offers a rare opportunity to see these magnificent prancing white steeds of Slovenia at their very best.

A dressage performance by a Lipizzaner. These famous white horses have been bred since 1580 in a farm in Lipica for the Spanish Riding School in Vienna, Austria.

FOOD

AGE-OLD PEASANT recipes, often requiring lengthy and intricate preparation, result in the most delicious Slovenian dishes. However, Slovenian meals have also been influenced by Austrian, Hungarian, German, Czech, Italian, and other Balkan styles of cooking. The result is a unique and cosmopolitan collection of culinary offerings. Visiting Slovenia in the year 2000, Anthony Dias Blue, editor of the international food magazine *Bon Appétit*, praised Slovenian cuisine as one of his "greatest discoveries."

PICNICS

At the first hint of warmer weather in the non-alpine areas of the country, Slovenian families pack a picnic basket and head for the woods, or the fields, or the banks of rivers. They may set up an outdoor barbecue or build an outdoor fire and toast or grill frankfurters or *klobasa* (kloh-bah-sah), which are large sausages that differ in their spiciness from region to region. If it's too hot to barbecue, picnickers will bring along sandwiches of local cheese and salami. Cheeses may vary greatly in consistency and taste from village to village. Sandwiches are usually made from fresh-baked bread, prepared either at home or in the brick ovens of a local bakery.

In addition to sandwiches, quick lunches of lighter repasts for hikers include the popular Slovenian snack bars, which come in a variety ranging from what we might term junk food to traditional and vegan health foods. Fresh fruit and raw vegetables are also popular trail foods.

For the uphill climber a *burek* (BOO-rek), a flaky pastry filled with cheese, is purchased from one of the many street kiosks found in both metropolitan areas and larger villages. These pastries can provide that needed spurt of energy to reach the top of the hill.

Opposite: **A street vendor selling beef goulash.**

BLACK KITCHENS

Throughout Slovenia, both in the Karavanke Mountains of the Savinjsko region and in the rural farm areas, home cooking, particularly baking, is done in the *crna kuhinja* (CERN-a KOO-hin-ya), or black kitchen (*below*). It is likely that the name comes from the fact that black kitchens traditionally had an open fireplace and no chimney, an arrangement resulting in a sooty film settling into the pores of the walls and counters. Possibly because of smoke, some black kitchens—but not all—are separate structures from the homes of the families for whom the food is being prepared.

Traditionally, in farm families it is the women who do the cooking while the men labor long hours in the fields. However, in cities, and even in many villages, as women claim their rightful place in Slovenian society more and more men are sharing the cooking and washing-up chores. Many younger Slovenian men take great pride in their innovative recipes.

Black kitchens, though, are still mainly the domain of rural women. Most feature old-fashioned wood-burning tile stoves (also known as Nuremberg stoves). The firebox inside the stove is lined with refractory bricks—bricks that can withstand very high temperatures. The upper body of the stove interior is made of ordinary bricks. The tiles on the outside of the stove hold in the heat and remain relatively cool to the touch. Some tile stoves are centuries old and are considered antiques. Stovecraft, the production of tiles for stoves, flourished as an art form in Slovenia and other middle European countries between 1870 and the late 1920s. Some of this work is still to be found in Slovenian black kitchens today.

BREAD, CAKES, AND PIES

The fame of black kitchens and wood-burning tile stoves was spread by the palate-pleasing breads, cakes, and pies produced in them. Bread is both a staple and a delicacy for Slovenes. Bread and rolls made in tile stoves are preferred for their texture and tastiness. Peasant breads, as they are known, tend to be crusted, grainy, and chewy. These breads come in many varieties, including whole wheat, rye, sourdough, and—a favorite in the Savinjsko region—traditional white-flour bread with a hard crust and softer, almost fluffy, center. Slovenian specialties include applesauce bread, grilled cinnamon bread, and shredded-wheat bread. An alternative to bread is savory muffins made of corn, wheat, or rice (often spread carefully with soft, farm-fresh butter or jam).

Freshly baked *pushti krofi*, or doughnuts, are enjoyed by many Slovenes.

Black kitchens also cater to the Slovenian sweet tooth. Among the uniquely Slovenian baked goods are *Jule* cake bursting with almonds and cherries, beautifully browned doughnuts made with nutmeg and sprinkled with sugar, sour cream twists, apple kuchen, apricot turnovers, Christmas plum pudding, and *kolachkee* (ko-LATCH-kee), or tart, filled with apricot jam or walnut paste.

Flacanti (FLAN-tza-ti) are traditional Slovenian cookies made with cinnamon, poppy seeds, or various jams. *Potica* (po-TEE-tza), with its variety of succulent ingredients layered in a meticulously prepared shell, is considered the Slovenian national cake. Pies of every kind—Bavarian chocolate, meringue, sweet potato, and all sorts of fruit in many styles of pie crusts— may be sampled in the different regions of Slovenia. Wild bilberry pie, made from a fruit native to the Balkans, offers a sweet-and-sour taste.

125

BILBERRIES, DANDELIONS, AND MUSHROOMS

An assortment of fresh mushrooms can be found at Slovenia's local markets. Slovenes also enjoy going into the forests to pick fresh wild mushrooms.

Carrying pails, buckets, jars, and baskets of all sizes, Slovenian adults and children of all ages take to the heaths and woods from July to September, when wild bilberry bushes produce their fruit. The shrubs are short and squat with wiry branches and globular leaves with a waxy surface. The berries are a blackish blue color and delicious when freshly picked. Although they are from the same family as blueberries, bilberries have a more pronounced flavor. They are often made into jams and jellies and preserved in large quantities to last through the autumn and winter. They can also be made into cookies or used as a filling for pies. Slovenes enjoy

a bilberry tea, and bilberry extract is both used as a dietary supplement and sold in health food stores for its medicinal qualities. These include preventing night blindness, strengthening eyesight, and counteracting simple diarrhea.

Before the bilberry-picking season opens, beginning in early spring, the hillsides in southern and central Slovenia draw hundreds of homemakers who engage in what appears to be stoop labor. They are picking wild dandelions or, to be more accurate, dandelion shoots. Bending over to peer at the sloped ground, these sharp-eyed pickers select only the very young plants, discarding the ones whose flowers are fully formed because their shoots will be bitter. There are several kinds of edible dandelions, and none are poisonous, but the ones with serrated leaves and whitish stems are the tastiest. These are used to make traditional Slovenian dandelion salad, a hearty dish prepared with peeled and sliced potatoes, hard-boiled eggs, chopped garlic, wine vinegar, lard with cracklings, and salt. A more modern version leaves out the lard and adds pumpkinseed and other vegetable oils.

The practice of foraging for wild mushrooms in Slovenia is so popular that it has been called a national sport. More than 70 varieties of edible mushrooms grow in the forests. Some of these have been so heavily picked that certain species are in danger of becoming extinct. To prevent this, legislation has been passed limiting how many can be plucked over a 24-hour period. Meaty, tasty mushrooms, low in calories and containing no fat, find their way into a wide variety of Slovenian dishes. They are eaten raw, as snacks; are ever present as garnishes for fowl, venison, and other meats; add flavor and body to a variety of stews; and are used as filling in a popular pastry sold by street vendors. Although strictly speaking, mushrooms are a fungus and not a vegetable, many Slovenes regard them as the tastiest vegetable of all.

Wine taverns can be found in the wine areas of Slovenia. Some taverns are located within the vineyards themselves and are popular places to taste the new wine.

BEVERAGES

Wines are drunk moderately with most dinner and lunch meals by many Slovenes. The regions of Podravje, Posavje, and Pomurje produce most of the wines of the country. The taste and bouquet of Slovenian wines varies from heavy red Bordeaux-style vintages and port wines to lighter and fruitier white chardonnays and dry sherries. Inexpensive table wines, which are also occasionally combined with sparkling water to make spritzers, include both white and red varieties. Among the most popular ones are such Slovenian whites as Malvazjia, a yellow-gold wine with a distinct bouquet and full taste, Bell pinot, a fruity white wine with a subtle bouquet, and Zelen, a light yellow-green wine reminiscent of green tea.

Beer halls in the cities of Slovenia serve a native *pivo* (PEE-vo), or beer, under the brand name *Lasko Zlatorog*, which is quite popular. They also serve *temino pivo* (TEM-no PEE-vo), or dark beer, which is a sort of stout. Available apertifs include *brinovec* (BRIE-no-vetz), which is a ginlike juniper-based liqueur; *slivovka* (SLEE-vow-ka), or plum brandy; *villijemovka* (VEE-liam-ow-ka), or pear brandy; and *sadjevec* (SAD-yea-vetz), which is a brandy made from a combination of fruits.

Kava (KA-va), or coffee, heads the list of nonalcoholic drinks that Slovenes prefer. In the home it's consumed black, or with sugar and milk or cream. In midafternoon, in the small café bars espresso and *cappucino* are preferred over ordinary coffee. *Caj* (CHAI), or tea, is usually served black, and tea variations such as pink tea and tea punch are popular. Also popular is a Slovenian punch made out of four kinds of fruit juice, crushed pineapple, and almond flavoring. Mineral water and carbonated beverages are also available. These are usually consumed with midafternoon pastry snacks or small, crustless sandwiches.

Cafés are popular venues to have coffee and cake.

SLOVENIAN GOULASH

This recipe makes six servings.

1 pound lean beef
1 pound (450 g) lean veal or 2 pounds (900 g) beef
3 tablespoons fat
1 large onion
1 teaspoons salt
1 teaspoon paprika
1 cup canned crushed tomatoes
8 small peeled potatoes

Cut meat in cubes and sauté with onion in hot fat, stirring occasionally to brown evenly. Add seasonings and tomatoes. Simmer about $1^1/_2$ hours or until meat is tender. Add potatoes after 1 hour of cooking; add more tomatoes if necessary. Serve hot.

POTICA

This recipe makes three or four loaves, depending on the size of the pan. To prepare the dough, very dry, high-quality, fine-grain wheat flour is often heated, preferably in a warm kitchen so that the yeast or dough will not "catch cold," preventing the potica from rising properly.

For the dough:
$^1/_2$ cup warm milk
2 ounces (57 g) yeast
1 tablespoon sugar
6 cups flour
$^1/_2$ cup butter, melted
1 teaspoon salt
3 eggs, beaten
$^1/_3$ cup sugar
1 cup sour cream (room temperature)

Nut filling:
1 $^1/_2$ cups heavy cream
$^1/_2$ cup butter
1 teaspoon vanilla
1 tablespoon brandy
1 $^1/_2$ pounds walnuts, ground
1 teaspoon cinnamon
$^1/_2$ teaspoon ground cloves
$^1/_3$ cup honey
3 egg yolks, slightly beaten
1 $^1/_2$ cups sugar
1 tablespoon sugar
1 tablespoon grated lemon rind
3 egg whites
1 tablespoon grated orange rind
3 cups yellow raisins (optional)

Dissolve yeast in warm milk. Add sugar and let stand in warm place until foamy. Place 5 cups flour into large bowl. Add salt, sugar, butter, eggs, sour cream, yeast mixture, and mix well. Add remaining flour and mix until dough separates from side of bowl. Knead until dough is pliant (about 10 minutes). If necessary, gradually add more flour. Place in greased bowl, cover with pastry cloth or cloth towel, and set aside in warm place to rise until doubled in bulk, about 1 hour. Scald cream with butter and pour over walnuts. Add the honey, sugar, grated lemon and orange rinds, vanilla, brandy, and cinnamon. Add 1 tablespoon sugar to the egg whites and beat until stiff. Fold egg whites into nut mixture and set aside. To assemble: Roll dough on lightly floured cloth to $^1/_4$-inch (0.6 cm) thickness. Spread nut mixture over rolled dough. Sprinkle the raisins over the nut mixture. Roll as for jelly roll. With seam edge down, place in well-greased loaf pans. Prick tops of loaves with a fork in several places. Cover with a light cloth and set aside in a warm place to rise, about 45 minutes. Brush top with beaten egg. Bake in 325°F (104°C) oven for approximately an hour. Remove pans from oven; leave poticas in pans for about 10 minutes, then remove and place on rack to cool.

AUSTRIA

A   B   C   D   E

1

2

●Ravne
Drava
●Maribor

●Slovenj Gradec

Kranjska Gora
Karanvanke Mountains

KOROSKA

Pohorje

Pannonian Hills

●Velenje

●**Ptuj**

▲Mount Triglav
(9,307 ft / 2,864 m)
●Jesenice
●Bled
Lake Bled

Julian Alps

Triglav National Park

PODRAVJE

SAVINGSKO

Savinja

●Kranj

●Celje

Kobarid

●Bohinj
Lake Bohinj

GORENJSKA

Soca

●Idrija

ZASAVJE
Zagorje●
Sava
●Trbovlje
●Hrastnik

3

ITALY

Soca Valley

GORISKA

LJUBLJANA●

CENTRAL SLOVENIA

POSAVJE

Sotla

●Nova Gorica

●Ajdovscina

●Vipava

Krsko
●Brezice

●Obrecje

4

PRIMORSKA

NOTRANJSKA

●Novo Mesto

Krka

Gorjanci Mountains

ADRIATIC

DOLENJSKA

SEA

●Koper
Piran● Izola●

5

Kolpa

F

HUNGARY

Murska Sobota

Slovenske Gorice

POMURJE

Mura

CROATIA

N

- ● Capital city
- ● Major town
- ▲ Mountain park

Feet	Meters
9,900	3,000
6,600	2,000
3,300	1,000
1,650	500
660	200
0	0

MAP OF SLOVENIA

Adriatic Sea, **A4–A5**
Ajdovscina, B4
Austria, A2–F1

Bled, B2
Bohinj, B3
Brezice, E4

Celje, D3
Central Slovenia, **B3–D3**
Croatia, A5–F2

Dolenjska, C4–D5
Drava (river), A1–F3

Gorenjska, A2–C3
Goriska, A2–B4
Gorjanci Mountains, **D4–E4**

Hrastnik, D3
Hungary, F1–F2

Idrija, B3
Italy, A2–B4
Izola, A5

Jesenice, B2
Julian Alps, A2–B2

Karavanke **Mountains,** **B2–C2**
Kobarid, A3
Kolpa (river), **C4–D5**

Koper, A5
Koroska, C2–D2
Kranj, B3
Krsko, D4

Lake Bled, B2
Lake Bohinj, B3
Ljubljana, C3

Maribor, E2

Mount Triglav, B2
Mura (river), D1–F2
Murska Sobota, F2

Notranjska, B4–C5
Nova Gorica, A3
Novo Mesto, D4

Obrecje, E4

Pannonian hills, E2
Piran, A5
Podravje, D2–F2
Pohorje Mountains, **E2**

Pomurje, E2–F2
Posavje, D3–E4
Primorska, A4–B5
Ptuj, E2

Ravne, D2

Sava (river), B3–F5
Savinja (river), C2– **D3**
Savinjsko, C2–E3
Slovenj Gradec, D2
Slovenske Gorice, **F2**
Soca (river), A3–A4
Sotla (river), E3–E4

Trbovlje, D3
Triglav National **Park, A2–B3**

Velenje, D2
Vipava, B4

Zagorje, D3
Zasavje, C3–D3

ECONOMIC SLOVENIA

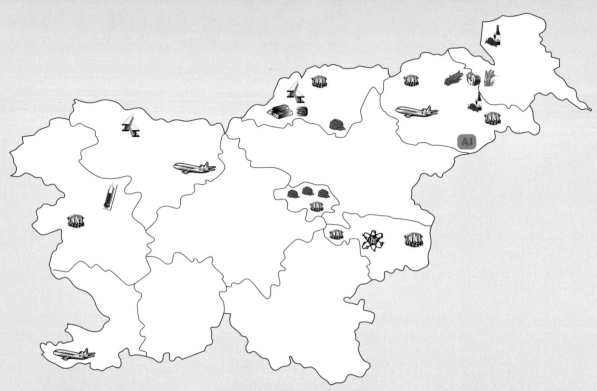

Agriculture

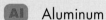 Corn

Dairy Products

Sugarbeets

Wheat

Wine

Naural Resources

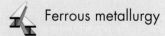 Aluminum

Coal

Hydroelectricity

Lead

Mercury

Nuclear reactor

Zinc

Services

Airport

Manufacturing

Ferrous metallurgy

ABOUT THE ECONOMY

OVERVIEW

Slovenia enjoys a very high per capita GDP. Privatization of the economy proceeded quickly in 2002. Steps were taken to bring the budget deficit down from 3 percent of GDP in 2002 to 1.9 percent in 2003. Despite the economic slowdown in Europe from 2001 to 2002, Slovenia maintained a 3-percent growth rate. A reformed business environment encourages foreign participation in the Slovenian economy. But inflation is a concern. Slovenia joined the European Union on May 1, 2004.

POPULATION

1,935,677 (2003 est.)

GROSS DOMESTIC PRODUCT

US$37.6 billion (2003 est.)

INFLATION RATE

7.4 percent (2002 est.)

CURRENCY

1 tolar (SIT) = 100 stotins
Notes: 10, 20, 50, 100, 200, 500, 1,000, 5,000, 10,000 tolar; coins: 1, 2, 5, 10, 20, 50 stotins
Stotin coins are issued in three denominations: 10, 20, and 50.
1 USD = 193 SIT (July 2004)
1 Euro (EUR) = 236 SIT (July 2004)

LAND USE

Irrigated land 4,942 acres (2001 ha) (1998 est.) Arable land 11.5 percent, permanent crops 2.7 percent, others 85.8 percent (1998 est.)

AGRICULTURAL PRODUCTS

Barley, corn, potatoes, soybeans, wheat, sugar beets; cattle, sheep, goats, pigs, poultry

NATURAL RESOURCES

Lignite coal, lead, zinc, mercury, uranium, silver, hydropower, forests

MAJOR EXPORTS

Manufactured goods, machinery and transportation equipment, chemicals, food

MAJOR IMPORTS

Manufactured goods, machinery and transportation equipment, chemicals, fuels and lubricants, food

MAIN TRADING PARTNERS

Germany, Italy, Croatia, Austria, France (2000)

EXTERNAL DEBT

US$7.9 billion (2001)

WORKFORCE

857,400

UNEMPLOYMENT RATE

11 percent

CULTURAL SLOVENIA

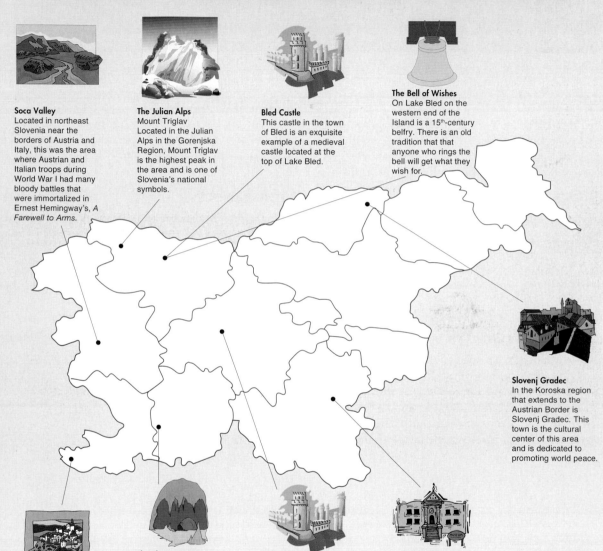

Soca Valley
Located in northeast Slovenia near the borders of Austria and Italy, this was the area where Austrian and Italian troops during World War I had many bloody battles that were immortalized in Ernest Hemingway's, *A Farewell to Arms.*

The Julian Alps
Mount Triglav Located in the Julian Alps in the Gorenjska Region, Mount Triglav is the highest peak in the area and is one of Slovenia's national symbols.

Bled Castle
This castle in the town of Bled is an exquisite example of a medieval castle located at the top of Lake Bled.

The Bell of Wishes
On Lake Bled on the western end of the Island is a 15th-century belfry. There is an old tradition that that anyone who rings the bell will get what they wish for.

Slovenj Gradec
In the Koroska region that extends to the Austrian Border is Slovenj Gradec. This town is the cultural center of this area and is dedicated to promoting world peace.

Piran
A beach town on the Adriatic Coast, picturesque Piran's old town is a treasure trove of Venetian gothic architecture with narrow streets.

The Skocjan Caves
In the middle of a larger area called *Kras* in Southern Slovenia is Divaca near the village where the caves are located. They are a labyrinth of caves and springs with an enormous canyon, underground caverns, and rivers.

Ljubljana Castle
Dating from1511 this castle, which is near the old town historical section of the major city in Slovenia, has spectacular views. It was rebuilt in 1511 after an earthquake. It has served as a royal residence and a prison.

Dolenjska Museum
This museum, located in Novo Mesto in the Dolenjska Region, south of Ljubijana, is a large complex that contains valuable archeological finds, as well as more modern collections.

ABOUT THE CULTURE

OFFICIAL NAME
Republika Slovenija (Republic of Slovenia)

CAPITAL
Ljubljana

DESCRIPTION OF FLAG
Three equal horizontal bands of white (top), blue, and red, with the Slovenian seal (a shield with the image of Triglav, Slovenia's highest peak, in white) against the blue background of the center band. Beneath the seal are two wavy blue lines depicting seas and rivers, and above it are three six-pointed stars arranged in an inverted triangle, taken from the coat of arms of the Counts of Celje, the great Slovene dynastic house of the late 14th and early 15th centuries. The seal is in the upper hoist side of the flag, centered in the white and blue bands.

LAND AREA
7,825 square miles (20,273 square km)

AGE STRUCTURE
0–14 years: 15.3 percent (male 152,341, female 144,189); 15–64 years: 70 percent (male 687,939, female 666,194); 65 years and over: 14.7 percent (male 105,837, female 179,177) (2003 est.)

POPULATION GROWTH RATE
0.14 percent (2003 est.)

BIRTH RATE
9.23 births per 1,000 people (2003 est.)

DEATH RATE
10.15 deaths per 1,000 people (2003 est.)

ETHNIC GROUPS
Slovene 88 percent, Croat 3 percent, Serb 2 percent, Bosniak 1 percent, Yugoslav 0.6 percent, Hungarian 0.4 percent, other 5 percent (2001)

RELIGIOUS GROUPS
Roman Catholic (Uniate) 57.8 percent, atheist 10.1 percent, unaffiliated believer 3.5 percent, Muslim 2.4 percent, Eastern Orthodox 2.3 percent, other Christian 1 percent, unknown 22.9 percent

LANGUAGES
Slovenian 91 percent, Serbo-Croatian 6 percent, other 3 percent

LITERACY RATE
99.7 percent (2003 est.)

NATIONAL HOLIDAYS
Independence/Statehood Day (June 25) celebrates the successful 1991 secession from Yugoslavia.

LEADERS IN POLITICS
Janez Drnovsek—president (2002–07)
Anton Rop—prime minister (2002–07)
Milan Kucan—former Communist, ran as an independent to become the first president of Slovenia in 1990 and led the country during its war of independence from Yugoslavia. Still very popular, he may run for president again in 2007.

TIME LINE

IN SLOVENIA	IN THE WORLD

300s B.C.
The lands that would become Slovenia, Croatia, and Bosnia-Herzegovina become part of the Roman Empire.

753 B.C.
Rome is founded.

116–17 B.C.
The Roman Empire reaches its greatest extent, under Emperor Trajan (98–17).

A.D. 500s
Ancestors of Slovenes settle in the Julian Alps.

A.D 623
King Samo establishes Slovenian kingdom.

A.D. 600
Height of Mayan civilization

1144
First records mention Ljubljana by name.

1000
The Chinese perfect gunpowder and begin to use it in warfare.

1300s
The Austro-Hungarian Habsburg Empire, rules Slovenia until 1918.

1550
The first book in Slovene, Catechisms, by Primoz Trubar, is printed.

1530
Beginning of trans-Atlantic slave trade organized by the Portuguese in Africa.

1558–1603
Reign of Elizabeth I of England

1584
The Bible is translated into Slovene by Jurij Dalmatin.

1620
Pilgrims sail the *Mayflower* to America.

1776
U.S. Declaration of Independence

1789–1799
The French Revolution

1838
First railway, part of the Vienna-Trieste route, is built in Slovenia.

1840s
"South Railway" between Celje and Ljubljana is built.

1861
The U.S. Civil War begins.

1869
Thirty thousand people rally at Vizmarje, near Ljubljana, to demand a united Slovenia.

1869
The Suez Canal is opened.

IN SLOVENIA	IN THE WORLD
1914 Slovenia, as part of the Austro-Hungarian Empire, enters World War I.	**1914** World War I begins.
1918 Slovenia becomes part of the Kingdom of Serbs, Croats, and Slovenes.	
1929 King Alexander I renames the country the Kingdom of Yugoslavia.	
	1939 World War II begins.
1945 Slovenia becomes a state of Communist Yugoslavia	**1945** The United States drops atomic bombs on Hiroshima and Nagasaki.
	1949 The North Atlantic Treaty Organization (NATO) is formed.
1955 Yugoslav dictator Tito and Soviet leader Nikita Khrushchev sign the Belgrade Declaration recognizing Yugoslavia as a Socialist state.	**1957** The Russians launch Sputnik.
	1966–1969 The Chinese Cultural Revolution
	1986 Nuclear power disaster at Chernobyl in Ukraine
1991 Slovenia declares its independence from Yugoslavia.	**1991** Break-up of the Soviet Union
1992 The United States and the European Union recognize Slovenia's independence. Slovenia joins the United Nations.	
	1997 Hong Kong is returned to China.
	2001 Terrorists crash planes in New York, Washington, D.C., and Pennsylvania.
2002 Slovenia is formally invited to join NATO	**2003** War in Iraq
2004 Slovenia joins the European Union.	

GLOSSARY

Black Kitchens or ***crna kuhinja*** (CERN-a HOO-hin-ya)
Kitchens with an open fireplace and no chimney where, in rural areas, traditional baking is still done.

despot
One who exercises power tyrannically.

Drzavni Zbor
Slovenian National Assembly; the legislative branch of the Slovenian government.

European Union (EU)
Organization of European countries dedicated to increasing economic integration and strengthening cooperation among its members. Slovenia joined the EU in 2004.

Germanization
The spread of German words and expressions that have become a part of everyday Slovene language.

Hapsburgs
The German royal family who ruled Austria from 1278 to 1918.

karst
A limestone area of underground caves, caverns and rivers.

Kurent
Carnival spirit; an early springtime figure born of pagan legend who allegedly worked his supernatural powers to chase winter away.

klobasa (klo-BA-sa)
sausage

laufarji
Masks that portray creatures in Slovenian myth, worn on Shrove Tuesday (40 days before Lent).

Lipizzaners
All-white performing horses of the royal Austrian court of the Hapsburgs, still performing today.

NATO
North Atlantic Treaty Organization.

potica (po-TEE-za)
The Slovenian national cake.

prince regent
A prince who governs a kingdom when the true ruler is a minor, absent or diabled.

Romany
A member of a traditionally itinerant group of people; gypsy.

tolar (TOH-lar)
The Slovenia monetary unit.

Trnfest (TERN-fest)
A five week program of cultural events held each August in Trnovo.

Yugoslavia
The nation that Slovenes, along with the Serbs and the Croats, formed in 1929.

FURTHER INFORMATION

BOOKS

Ashworth, Susie. *Central Europe*. Oakland, CA: Lonely Planet, 2003.

Benderly, Jill and Evan Kraft, eds. *Independent Slovenia: Origins, Movements, Prospects*. New Jersey: Distributor a1Books (Publisher, PRAV), 1996.

Fallon, Steve. *Slovenia*. Oakland, CA: Lonely Planet, 2004.

Gow, James and Kathie Carmichael. *Slovenia and the Slovenes*. Bloomington: Indiana University Press, 2000.

Langley, Norm. *The Rough Guide to Slovenia*. NY: Rough Guides limited, 2004.

Peoples of Europe. NY: Marshall Cavendish, 2003.

Portis-Winner and Irene. *Semiotics of Peasants in Transition: Slovenia Villagers and Their Ethnic Relatives in America*. Durham, NC: Duke University Press, 2002.

Roberts, J.M. *The Illustrated History of the World*. NY: Oxford University Press, 2001.

Sinkovec, Bostjan. *Cornerstones: Of Slovenia's NATO Membership*. Lincoln, NE: Universe, Inc., 2003.

Vidstrup Monk, Karin ed. *Central Europe Phrasebook*. Oakland, CA: Lonely Planet, 2001.

Zawacki, Andrew. *Afterwards: Slovenian Writing, 1945–1995*. Buffalo, NY: White Pine Press, 1999.

WEBSITES

Banke Slovenije (Bank of Slovenia). www.bsi.si/html/eng/index.html

Central Intelligence Agency World Factbook (select "Slovenia" from the country list) www.cia.gov/cia/publications/factbook/geos/si.html

Lonely Planet World Guide: Slovenia. www.lonelyplanet.com/destinations/europe/slovenia

Matkurja—A Guide to Virtual Slovenia. www.matkurja.com/eng/country-info

Republic of Slovenia Public Relations and Media Office. www.uvi.si/eng

Slovenian Tourist Board. www.slovenia-tourism.si/

U.S. Department of State. www.state.gov/p/eur/ci/si

VIDEOS

Rick Stevens' Europe: Bulgaira, Eastern Turkey, Slovenia, and Croatia. Europe Through the Back Door, 2000.

FILMS

Oda Preserenu (Ode to the Poet) is about Slovenia's greatest cultural hero, the romantic poet France Preseren. With English subtitles, it was directed by Martin Srebotnjak, 2001.

BIBLIOGRAPHY

BOOKS
Fallon, Steve and Neil Wilson. *Lonely Planet Slovenia*. 3rd ed. London: Lonely Planet Publications, 2001.
Glenny, Misha. *The Fall of Yugoslavia*. Revised. New York: Penguin Books, 1993.
Gow, James and Kathie Carmichael. *Slovenia and the Slovenes*. Bloomington, IN: Indiana University Press, 2000.
Ramet, Sabrina P. *Gender Politics in the Western Balkans: Women and Society in Yugoslavia and the Yugoslav Successor States (Post-Communist Cultural Studies)*. University Park: Penn State University Press, 1999.
Rogel, Carole. *The Slovenes and Yugoslavism, 1890-1914*. New York: East European Quarterly, 1977.

WEBSITES
Republic of Slovenia Public Relations and Media Office. www.uvi.si/eng
Central Intelligence Agency (CIA)—The World Factbook: Slovenia
www.cia.gov/cia/publications/factbook/geos/si.html

INDEX